The battle on the Death Star.

LIFE

George Lucas and the Making of Star Wars

EDITORIAL DIRECTOR Kostya Kennedy
EDITOR/WRITER J.I. Baker
DIRECTOR OF PHOTOGRAPHY Christina Lieberman
ART DIRECTOR Lan Yin Bachelis
COPY CHIEF Parlan McGaw
COPY EDITOR Joel Van Liew
PICTURE EDITOR Rachel Hatch
WRITER-REPORTER Daniel S. Levy
PHOTO ASSISTANT Steph Durante
PRODUCTION DESIGN Sandra Jurevics
PREMEDIA TRAFFICKING SUPERVISOR Paige E. King
DIRECTOR, PREMEDIA QUALITY SERVICES Dale Tunender

MEREDITH SPECIAL INTEREST MEDIA
VICE PRESIDENT & GROUP PUBLISHER Scott Mortimer
VICE PRESIDENT, GROUP EDITORIAL DIRECTOR Stephen Orr
VICE PRESIDENT, MARKETING Jeremy Biloon
EXECUTIVE ACCOUNT DIRECTOR Doug Stark
DIRECTOR, BRAND MARKETING Jean Kennedy
ASSOCIATE DIRECTOR, BRAND MARKETING Bryan Christian
SENIOR BRAND MANAGER Katherine Barnet

EDITORIAL DIRECTOR Kostya Kennedy
CREATIVE DIRECTOR Gary Stewart
DIRECTOR OF PHOTOGRAPHY Christina Lieberman
EDITORIAL OPERATIONS DIRECTOR Jamie Roth Major
MANAGER, EDITORIAL OPERATIONS Gina Scauzillo

SPECIAL THANKS Brad Beatson, Melissa Frankenberry, Samantha Lebofsky, Kate Roncinske, Laura Villano

MEREDITH NATIONAL MEDIA GROUP
PRESIDENT Jon Werther
PRESIDENT, MEREDITH MAGAZINES Doug Olson
PRESIDENT, CONSUMER PRODUCTS Tom Witschi
PRESIDENT, CHIEF DIGITAL OFFICER Catherine Levene
CHIEF REVENUE OFFICER Michael Brownstein
CHIEF MARKETING & DATA OFFICER Alysia Borsa
MARKETING & INTEGRATED COMMUNICATIONS Nancy Weber

SENIOR VICE PRESIDENTS
CONSUMER REVENUE Andy Wilson
CORPORATE SALES Brian Kightlinger
DIRECT MEDIA Patti Follo
RESEARCH SOLUTIONS Britta Cleveland
STRATEGIC SOURCING, NEWSSTAND, PRODUCTION Chuck Howell
DIGITAL SALES Marla Newman
THE FOUNDRY Matt Petersen
PRODUCT & TECHNOLOGY Justin Law

VICE PRESIDENTS
FINANCE Chris Susil
BUSINESS PLANNING & ANALYSIS Rob Silverstone
CONSUMER MARKETING Steve Crowe
BRAND LICENSING Steve Grune
CORPORATE COMMUNICATIONS Jill Davison

VICE PRESIDENT, GROUP EDITORIAL DIRECTOR Stephen Orr
DIRECTOR, EDITORIAL OPERATIONS & FINANCE Greg Kayko

MEREDITH CORPORATION
PRESIDENT & CHIEF EXECUTIVE OFFICER Tom Harty
CHIEF FINANCIAL OFFICER Joseph Ceryanec
CHIEF DEVELOPMENT OFFICER John Zieser
CHIEF STRATEGY OFFICER Daphne Kwon
PRESIDENT, MEREDITH LOCAL MEDIA GROUP Patrick McCreery
SENIOR VICE PRESIDENT, HUMAN RESOURCES Dina Nathanson

CHAIRMAN Stephen M. Lacy
VICE CHAIRMAN Mell Meredith Frazier

Published by LIFE Books, an imprint of Meredith Corporation • 225 Liberty Street • New York, NY 10281

PRINTED IN THE USA

FRONT COVER: George Lucas and Anthony Daniels (as C-3PO) on the Tunisian set of *Star Wars,* 1977.
BACK COVER: Mark Hamill as Luke Skywalker in *Star Wars.*

Contents

Harrison Ford as Han Solo in *Star Wars*.

INTRODUCTION

Hollywood Wars

THE BLUEPRINT FOR THE MODERN BLOCKBUSTER, STAR WARS BEGAN AS A PERSONAL—AND RISKY—FILM FOR YOUNG GEORGE LUCAS

A LONG TIME AGO IN A GALAXY FAR, FAR away—well, America in the 1970s—pessimism reigned. The nightmare of the Vietnam War, the disgrace of the Watergate scandal, and the economic disaster of the energy crisis had turned the idealistic high of the 1960s into the hangover of the Me Decade. American movies reflected this zeitgeist with such downbeat films as *Cabaret, The Conversation,* and *Chinatown.* On screen and off, it seemed the bad guys had won.

George Lucas's first feature, the dystopian *THX 1138,* was no exception. When the film bombed at the box office in 1971, Lucas's wife, Marcia, suggested that he shift gears. Why not make a film that would make audiences laugh and cry? Why not make a movie with heart? The suggestion inspired Lucas's *American Graffiti,* a nostalgic ode to the director's automotive adolescence. After it became a hit in 1973, Lucas dug even deeper into his past, finding inspiration in his childhood love of science fiction.

The result was *Star Wars.* In marked contrast to the cynicism of the day, the story of Luke Skywalker, a humble farm boy who becomes an intergalactic hero, was almost absurdly upbeat, even naive, reveling in comic book gee-whizzery and what Lucas called "effervescent giddiness." Partly because of this quality, most of Lucas's filmmaking friends hated the movie. *Star Wars'* studio, 20th Century Fox, was certain it would fail. Even Lucas expected a disaster.

In the end, *Star Wars* broke all box office records and became a bona fide cultural phenomenon—a success largely driven by nostalgia for a more innocent age. "Someone had gone and spent umpteen millions of dollars lovingly and faithfully putting on screen the science fiction of my youth—from the opening title taken from a *Flash Gordon*–style Saturday serial to a bar just like the bars that pulp writers employed not only in SF but in mysteries and cowboy tales as well," the novelist John Crowley, a three-time winner of the World Fantasy Award, tells LIFE. "It was impossible not to laugh with delight at every corny labor-of-love moment."

Star Wars was corny but also funny, exhilarating, and suspenseful. It made people laugh and cry. In the estimation of the *Washington Post,* the movie "helped close some of the psychological wounds left by the war in Vietnam." More than anything, *Star Wars,* as Lucas intended, was a film with heart. That meant it was built to last—and last it certainly has, a nine-part saga told over a span of 42 years. Auxiliary blockbusters. A multitude of media and marketing platforms. A rousing and unfettered afterlife. Over that long time, America, George Lucas, and *Star Wars* have come a far, far way. And still, as ever, the good guys win. ●

MARK HAMILL (LUKE Skywalker), Carrie Fisher (Princess Leia), and George Lucas on the set of *Star Wars*. The actors frequently found it difficult to say Lucas's chewy dialogue, but he didn't like it when they ad-libbed. "This is all very real and very serious," Lucas told Fisher after she changed one of her lines.

Desert Chic

George Lucas was 31 years old when he began directing *Star Wars* on location in Tunisia. He wrapped the scarf over his face (and covered his Panavision cameras in plastic) to protect against blowing sand, which got into everything. Despite the precautions, one camera lens was damaged. Location filming was painfully slow—it took Lucas three days to capture the now-famous shot of Luke staring dreamily into the sunset on Tatooine.

Behind the Scenes

THE PATH OF GEORGE LUCAS, AND *STAR WARS*, IN CANDID PHOTOS

Science Friction

Star Wars' X-34 landspeeder had a small car inside, so that Mark Hamill (Luke Skywalker) could actually drive it. Hamill is shown here in the driver's seat during a break in shooting, along with Alec Guinness (Obi-Wan Kenobi, right) as well as Anthony Daniels (C-3PO, behind Hamill) and an unidentified stormtrooper without the iconic headgear.

DANIELS

Empire Builders

Hamill (left), Lucas, Carrie Fisher, and Harrison Ford on the set of 1980's *The Empire Strikes Back*. *Star Wars* had made all of them major stars. Only Hamill and Fisher were contractually obligated to do the sequel, and Ford refused to get on board unless his character was given more substance. He also received a share of the film's gross and merchandising profits.

Covenant Colleagues

Lucas and Steven Spielberg on the set of 1981's *Raiders of the Lost Ark*. The filmmakers originally wanted Tom Selleck to play Indiana Jones, but the actor had signed on to play the titular character in the CBS series *Magnum, P.I.* In the end, they settled for their second choice: Harrison Ford.

Back at the Ranch

The Lucasfilm archives at Lucas's Skywalker Ranch in Marin County, California, store such items as Chewbacca's head, C-3PO, R2-D2, Indiana Jones's hat and whip, and the Ark of the Covenant—all shown in this photo taken by Taryn Simon for her series *An American Index of the Hidden and Unfamiliar*, 2007.

fragile
FRAGILE
THIS WAY UP
FRAGILE
JAK

CHAPTER 1

A Shooting Star

HOW AN ASPIRING RACE-CAR DRIVER NAMED GEORGE LUCAS HELPED TRANSFORM HOLLYWOOD

A YOUNG LUCAS IN MODESTO, California, in 1968. "I was very much aware that growing up wasn't pleasant. It was just . . . frightening. I remember that I was unhappy a lot of the time. Not really unhappy—I enjoyed my childhood. But I guess all kids, from their point of view, feel depressed and intimidated."

EARLY 1977 WAS NOT A good time for George Lucas. *Star Wars,* the 32-year-old director's troubled science fiction film, seemed destined to fail. After laboring over the script for years and enduring a grueling four-month shoot that brought him to the brink of a nervous breakdown, Lucas decided to show a rough cut of the film to his friends—including directors Brian De Palma, Martin Scorsese, and Steven Spielberg, and *Time* magazine's film critic, Jay Cocks.

Held that February at Lucas's home in San Anselmo, California, the screening was—to put it mildly—a disaster. "When the film ended, people were aghast," said its producer, Gary Kurtz. The reaction was so bad that Lucas's wife, Marcia—the film's editor—burst into tears. "It's awful," she sobbed.

It got worse. "We all got into these cars to go somewhere for lunch," said Gloria Katz, a writer who had worked with Lucas, "and in our car everyone was saying, 'My God, what a disaster.'" De Palma was particularly savage, taking Lucas to task for Princess Leia's hair buns ("What are those, Danish pastries?"), the film's quasi spirituality ("What's all this Force s--t?'"), its lack of realism ("Where's the blood when they shoot people?"), and the villain Darth Vader ("That's the best you can do?"). "Brian wouldn't let up," Katz said. "He was like a crazed dog."

The sole enthusiast was Spielberg, whose smash hit *Jaws* had established the paradigm-changing concept of the summer blockbuster just two years before. "That movie is going to make $100 million," he told his friends, "and I'll tell you why: It has a marvelous innocence and naivete in it, which is George, and people will love it." Later, Spielberg told Alan Ladd Jr., the 20th Century Fox executive who had staked his career on the film, that *Star Wars* would make a "fortune."

Hollywood insiders disagreed with Spielberg's assessment. The word on the street was that the big summer movies would be William Friedkin's *Sorcerer,* a remake of the 1953 classic *The Wages of Fear,* and *The Other Side of Midnight,* a lurid melodrama based on Sidney Sheldon's best-selling 1973 novel. How could a larky science fiction film compete with these "surefire" hits? Increasingly, the answer seemed to be "It can't." Theater audiences were booing the *Star Wars* trailer, after all, and Lucas himself remained disappointed with his film.

IN 1962, LUCAS WAS A member of the Thomas Downey High School tennis team in Modesto (this page), a small central California town, shown opposite in the 1950s. "My family came from nowhere," Lucas once said. "Nobody knows where we originally came from."

But he couldn't postpone the inevitable, and the film's first public screening was scheduled for May 1, 1977, at San Francisco's Northpoint Theatre.

Lucas's career was on the line. If the prevailing sentiment was correct and his film tanked, would he be forced to eke out a living making low-rent documentaries, abandoning the grand artistic ambitions he'd nurtured since his early film-school days? It was a dispiriting prospect for a man who'd felt he was destined for greatness ever since a car crash changed his life at age 18.

BORN IN MODESTO, CALIFORNIA, on May 14, 1944, George Lucas—the third of four children born to Dorothy, a housewife, and George Sr., the owner of a stationery store—was a bright, if often unfocused, child. "I daydreamed a lot," he said. "I was always described as somebody who could be doing a lot better than I was doing, not working up to potential. I was so bored."

Like many teenagers, Lucas escaped into the fantasy worlds of comic books and the novels of such authors as Arthur Conan Doyle, whose *Lost World* Lucas would later call his favorite book. With the rise of television, Lucas became obsessed with *Flash Gordon,* a science fiction series that premiered in 1954. In the end, TV would influence Lucas far more than film. "Movies had extremely little effect on me when I was growing up," he said. "I hardly ever went, and when I did it was to meet girls."

The young man's other great interest—cars—was yet another way to mingle with the opposite sex. The teenage Lucas spent his evenings cruising Modesto's 10th and 11th Streets as he listened to rock 'n' roll—particularly the music played by the enigmatic disc jockey Wolfman Jack. "I started driving at 15," he later said. "But once I was 16, I got my license and I could really drive around, out on the streets, and I kind of got lost in cruising from that point on—cars were all-consuming to me."

Though George Sr. expected his only son to take over his business, George Jr. had other plans. In fact, he had his heart set on a car-racing career, until the evening of June 12, 1962, three days before Lucas's high school graduation. The young man was driving home in his Fiat Bianchina when he was blindsided by a classmate's car. "He was doing 80 or 90 miles an hour, showing off and trying to pass me," Lucas said. "I never saw him. He hit me broadside just as I was turning into our drive." Lucas's car flipped over "seven or eight times," Lucas said, throwing him onto the road before it smashed into a walnut tree. Hearing the noise, Dorothy went outside to find her badly injured son lying unconscious on the ground.

Though Lucas had narrowly avoided death, he wasn't out of the woods. He began vomiting blood in the ambulance on the way to the hospital and eventually slipped into a coma. After regaining consciousness 48 hours later, he experienced a life-changing awakening. "I realized more than anything else what a thin thread we hang on in life," he later said. "I was

LUCAS IN HIS SENIOR YEAR AT Thomas Downey High School (this page). Opposite: The cover of a 1930s edition of *The Warlord of Mars* by Edgar Rice Burroughs. Best known for his stories about Tarzan, Burroughs also wrote novels about swashbuckling space heroes that captivated Lucas and became an influence on *Star Wars*.

in an accident that, in theory, no one could survive. So it was like, 'Well, I'm here, and every day now is an extra day. I've been given an extra day so I've got to make the most of it.'"

Not surprisingly, the experience changed Lucas's perspective on racing. "You see what the future is there, and you realize that you'll probably end up being dead," he said. "And I just decided that maybe that wasn't for me." In short, he was "going to have to figure out something else to do."

At first, that "something else" was an emphasis on education. After two weeks in the hospital—he essentially graduated from high school while recovering in bed—and months in rehab, Lucas enrolled in Modesto Junior College to study anthropology, sociology, and psychology. "For the first time, I was into something I really cared about and my whole grade situation just turned around," he said. "I had thought I was a terrible student, and then suddenly I was a great student."

At the same time, he was developing an interest in the visual arts and might have gone on to attend Pasadena's Art Center College of Design, if his father hadn't forbidden it. "I'm not going to pay for that," George Sr. warned. "Do it on your own if you want. You'll never make a living as an artist."

Then, a friend told Lucas about the cinema department at the University of Southern California (USC), one of the first colleges in the country to offer such classes. "I thought that was insane," Lucas said. "I didn't know that you could go to college to learn how to make movies." He applied.

Though he'd given up racing for good, Lucas had begun filming cars with an 8mm camera—a gift from his father. Some of his early efforts featured Allen Grant, a driver whom Lucas had met at the Laguna Seca racetrack, not far from Modesto. Lucas had briefly worked as a mechanic for Grant, who was friends with Haskell Wexler, the noted cinematographer and racing enthusiast.

Best known for his work on such classic films as *Who's Afraid of Virginia Woolf?* (1966) and *In the*

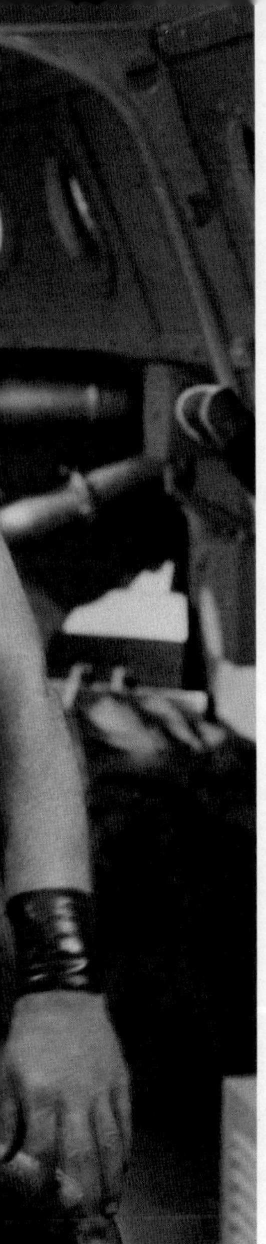

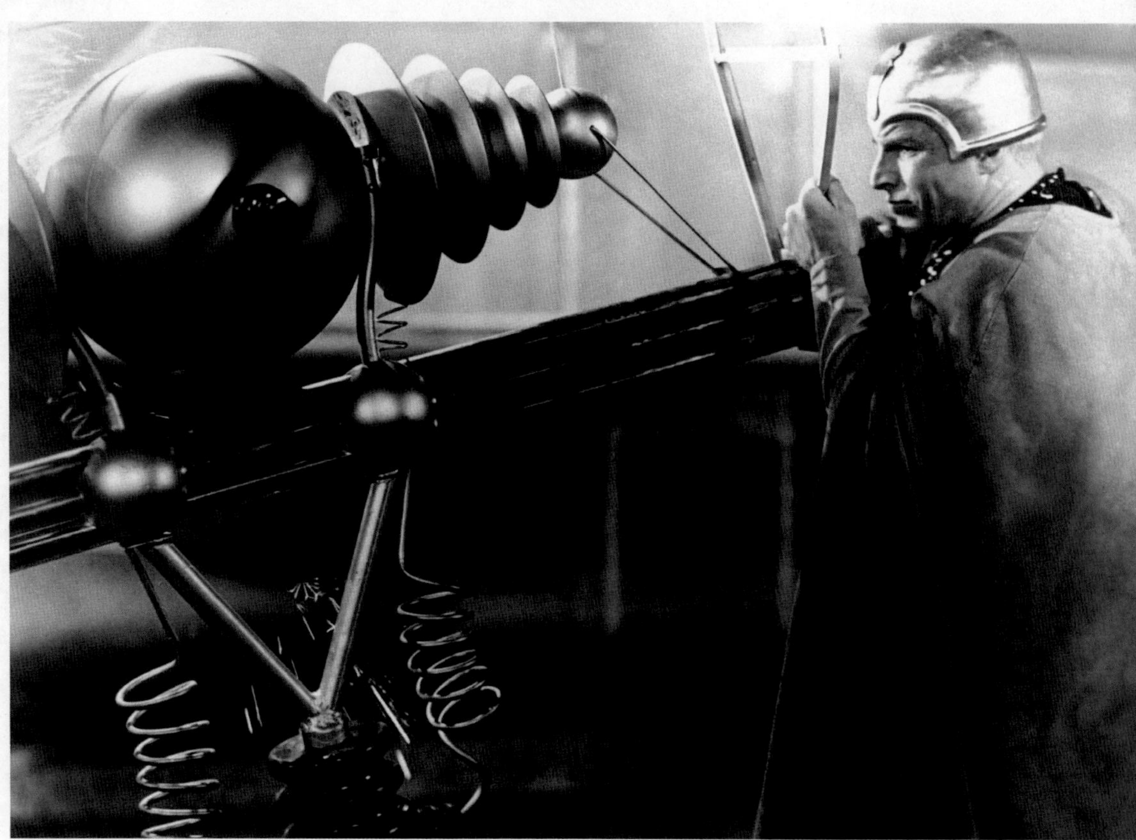

STAR WARS ORIGINATED WITH Lucas's desire to make a big-budget version of *Flash Gordon*, a superhero franchise that originated in a 1934 comic strip by Alex Raymond. It branched out into movies, such as 1938's *Flash Gordon's Trip to Mars*, shown in the photos above, and later, television.

Heat of the Night (1967), Wexler was at the track and Grant introduced him to Lucas, who told him of his interest in film. Impressed with the young man's enthusiasm, Wexler called a USC faculty member. "For God's sake, keep an eye on this kid," he said. "He's got the calling."

Those words from Wexler may have been what opened the door at USC. "I got accepted!" Lucas said. This time, George Sr. didn't object—probably because he had no idea what cinematography was. "He didn't care as long as I wasn't in the art department," Lucas said.

Around the time that Oliver Stone and Martin Scorsese were studying film at New York University and Francis Ford Coppola was at UCLA and Steven Spielberg attended Long Beach State, Lucas was settling in at USC. He became part of a cabal affectionately dubbed the USC Mafia, a.k.a. the Dirty Dozen, whose members included future writer-director John Milius (*Conan the Barbarian*) and director Randal Kleiser (*Grease, The Blue Lagoon*). "I discovered the school of cinema was really about making movies," Lucas later said.

It was also about learning from established directors. During his time at USC, Lucas was particularly impressed with the films of Akira Kurosawa, the Japanese director who had, in turn, been inspired by Hollywood's John Ford—a hall of mirrors of cross-cultural influences. Lucas was particularly taken with Kurosawa's 1958 film, *The Hidden Fortress,* the story of two squabbling peasants who fall under the influence of a mysterious man and help rescue a princess—characters who would eventually help inspire R2-D2, C-3PO, Obi-Wan Kenobi, and Princess Leia in *Star Wars.*

Lucas also loved Kurosawa's 1954 classic, *Seven Samurai,* and its 1960 Hollywood remake, *The Magnificent Seven.* "It really had a huge influence on my life in terms of seeing something that brilliant and something that emotional, and at the same time so exotic," Lucas said.

At USC, the young man also fell under the spell of professors Lester

"I ASSUMED I WOULD MAKE THE KIND OF AVANT-GARDE FILMS THAT WERE BEING MADE IN SAN FRANCISCO AT THE TIME."

—GEORGE LUCAS

Novros and Slavko Vorkapich, who emphasized a nonnarrative approach to film. More than anything, Lucas wanted to make small, personal, edgy, experimental work. "I assumed I would make the kind of avant-garde films that were being made in San Francisco at the time," he said—an ironic ambition for a man whose so-called "popcorn movies" would permanently transform popular culture.

Lucas's first USC film, 1965's *Look at LIFE,* was a montage of images from LIFE magazine, but his breakthrough came in 1967 with his graduate project, *THX 1138 4EB.* The 15-minute dystopian science fiction film showcased Lucas's sophisticated, innovative sense of imagery and sound. "I was trying to create emotions through pure cinematic techniques," he said. "All the films I made during that time center on conveying emotions through a cinematic experience, not necessarily through the narrative. Throughout my career, I've remained a cinema enthusiast; even though I went on to make films with a more conventional narrative, I've always tried to convey emotions through essentially cinematic experiences."

THX 1138 4EB received a rapturous reception at a USC student film festival. Even Lucas's father was impressed. "We guessed he had finally found his niche," George Sr. said. "As we drove home, I said to Dorothy, 'I think we put our money on the right horse.'" One of the film's biggest fans was another would-be filmmaker named Steven Spielberg. "There was so much virtuosity in the craft and the vision and the emotion of that story," he said. "It absolutely stopped the festival. You could have heard a pin drop in that theater."

Thanks to *THX 1138 4EB*'s success, Lucas won a scholarship to make a short documentary about the filming of Columbia Pictures' 1969 western *MacKenna's Gold.* The experience proved to be dispiriting for Lucas ("Watching doesn't teach you anything," he grumbled), but he remained determined to gain a foothold in Hollywood. Before long, another scholarship put him on the Burbank set of Warner Bros.–Seven Arts' *Finian's Rainbow,* the film adaptation of an outdated 1947 Broadway musical.

In the late 1960s, the movie business was floundering after the collapse of the old-line studio system. "In the past, studios had owned production facilities to make the movies, distribution companies to send them out for exhibition, and—conveniently—the theaters to show their own films in," says Ed Sikov, a noted film scholar and the author of *On Sunset Boulevard: The Life and Times of Billy Wilder.* That all changed in 1948, when the United States won a lawsuit against Paramount Pictures that limited the studio's ability to monopolize distribution. "The ruling tore the studio system apart," Sikov adds.

The growing popularity of television didn't help. Desperately trying to compete with the new medium, Hollywood studios began churning out overblown, uninspired epics—a trend epitomized by 1963's *Cleopatra,* a $35 million plus spectacle starring Elizabeth Taylor. "Some of these films were very successful, like *The Sound of*

RACE-CAR ENTHUSIAST LUCAS (above, at right, in Laguna Seca, and left, riding shotgun in Santa Barbara) crewed for noted driver Allen Grant (behind the wheel in both photos) in 1963. Grant became the model for the character of John Milner (Paul Le Mat) in Lucas's *American Graffiti* (1973). "Allen Grant was my hero," Lucas said.

Music, with Julie Andrews," Sikov says. "Even *Cleopatra* made its money back. But some of them were over-budget busts, like Richard Fleischer's *Doctor Dolittle,* Billy Wilder's *The Private Life of Sherlock Holmes,* Robert Wise's *Star!* and Blake Edwards's *Darling Lili.*"

Finian's Rainbow was no exception. Once again, Lucas was unimpressed with what he saw. "I wasn't really interested," said Lucas, who nevertheless found an important friend and mentor in the director of *Finian's Rainbow*: a 28-year-old named Francis Ford Coppola.

A **GRADUATE OF THE THEATER** department at Hofstra University and UCLA's film program, Coppola had made rapid inroads into the movie business—thanks to his confidence, charisma, and talent for both writing and directing. "In those years, it was unheard of for a young fellow to make a feature film," he said. "I was the first one." His debut as a mainstream writer-director, 1963's *Dementia 13,* was a surprisingly effective low-budget black-and-white horror film. Before long, Coppola was in demand as a writer, eventually winning an Academy Award for the screenplay for 1970's *Patton.*

The two filmmakers were "good friends right from the moment we met," Lucas said. This was partly because they were both in their twenties—a rarity in 1960s Hollywood—and formed a complementary union of opposites: Where Lucas was reserved and methodical, Coppola was impulsive and brash—not to mention a compulsive womanizer. He'd even hit on Marcia Lucas, née Griffin, the film editor whom Lucas had met while studying at USC and married

THE TWO SQUABBLING peasants (above) in Akira Kurosawa's *The Hidden Fortress* (1958) inspired C-3PO and R2-D2 in *Star Wars* (opposite). "I grew up in a small town in central California, and the movie theaters didn't show much beyond *The Bridge on the River Kwai* and *The Blob,*" Lucas said, "so I didn't really experience foreign films until I found my way into film school."

LUCAS WAS DEEPLY influenced by the work of Kurosawa, who is shown on the set of 1980's *Kagemusha* (opposite, bottom, at left) with Francis Ford Coppola (center) and Lucas, both of whom served as executive producers on the film. Kurosawa's *Seven Samurai* (above) was remade in Hollywood as 1960's *The Magnificent Seven* (opposite, top)—another important influence on *Star Wars*.

in February 1969. "He was constantly jumping off cliffs," Lucas said, "and I was always shouting 'Don't do it, you'll get yourself killed!'"

The flip side of Coppola's recklessness was his galvanic vision. He wanted nothing less than to transform the movie business by establishing his own cinematic satellite in San Francisco. "We could make movies anywhere in the world," he told Lucas. "We don't have to be in Hollywood."

Calling his fledgling company American Zoetrope, he made Lucas his executive vice president in early 1969—just one of many opportunities he gave the younger man. "He taught me how to write screenplays, taught me how to work with actors," Lucas said. "I was much more of a cameraman and a film editor, much more on the technical side of things."

Coppola hired Lucas to work on *Finian's Rainbow* and then had him document the making of his next film, 1969's *The Rain People,* about a pregnant woman who goes on the road with a handsome hitchhiker. Lucas called his 1968 documentary about the shoot *Filmmaker.*

Not long after *The Rain People* wrapped, Coppola decided that Lucas should direct a feature version of *THX 1138 4EB.* Lucas's student film had steadily grown in stature, winning prizes at festivals and impressing almost everyone who saw it. Not surprisingly, the moribund Hollywood studios didn't share this enthusiasm: Why would they want to bankroll a downbeat, experimental film from an unproven director?

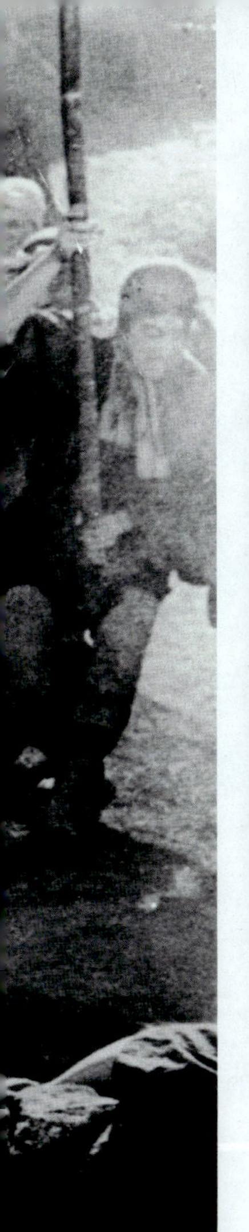

That attitude changed—along with the rest of Hollywood—when *Easy Rider* was released in July 1969. Co-written by Terry Southern (*Dr. Strangelove*) and actors Peter Fonda and Dennis Hopper, *Easy Rider* followed rebel bikers on a drug-fueled road trip from Mexico to New Orleans. Made outside of the studio system for a mere $350,000, the film (produced by Fonda and directed by Hopper) became one of the most successful movies ever made—and yet another nail in the coffin of Old Hollywood. "There was a breakthrough with *Easy Rider,* which finally suggested to the studios that there might be something to the way we were thinking," said Walter Murch, *The Rain People's* sound editor. Partly as a result of *Easy Rider's* success, Coppola convinced Warner Bros. to loan him $300,000 for *THX 1138* and other projects and an additional $300,000 to establish American Zoetrope. "Francis could sell ice to the Eskimos," Lucas said. "He has charisma beyond logic. I can see now what kind of men the great Caesars of history were, their magnetism."

One of the projects percolating at American Zoetrope was *Apocalypse Now,* a film based on Joseph Conrad's 1902 novella, *Heart of Darkness,* set in the context of the Vietnam War. "George and I would talk about the battles and what a great movie it would make," said John Milius, whom Coppola had hired to write the script. "He loved it because of all the technology, the helicopters, air strikes by Phantoms, the night-vision scopes, and devices to detect people walking around at night."

First, Lucas had to finish *THX 1138*. After struggling with multiple drafts of the script in his Mill Valley, California, home ("I hate writing," he said), Lucas started filming in San Francisco on September 22, 1969, and ended nearly two months later. Most of the film was made on the fly. "We barely got into some of the locations," Lucas said. "Sometimes we'd only have about two hours to shoot in a particular place. There were a lot of things that made it feel like a street film—we would get in there, get our shots before the police came, and then run away as fast as we could."

Set in a future civilization where conformity is the rule and individuality a crime, the film focuses on THX 1138 (Robert Duvall), a normally dutiful citizen whose perspective begins to change when he stops taking mandated mind-control drugs. "My vision was not to do a normal story," Lucas said. "I wanted to do something that was abstract, much more like a student film than like a drama. Obviously, to get it through the studios, it had to be a drama, but by this time *Easy Rider* had come out, so we thought, 'Maybe we can get away with a really wacky avant-garde film.' I said, 'This is probably the only chance I'll ever get to do something like this.'"

He was right. On November 19, 1970—a day that would become known as Black Thursday—Coppola showed Warner Bros. the final edit of *THX 1138*. The screening was an unmitigated disaster. "It was insane," Lucas said. "I wish I had filmed it. It was like bringing an audience to the *Mona Lisa* and asking, 'Do you know why she's smiling?' 'Sorry, Leonardo, you'll have to go back and make some changes.'"

That's exactly what Warner Bros. executives demanded—except they didn't trust Lucas or Coppola to recut the film, so they gave it to a house editor instead. The disappointment of *THX 1138*—combined with the financial failure of *The Rain People*—led Warner Bros. to demand their money back from Coppola. Determined to

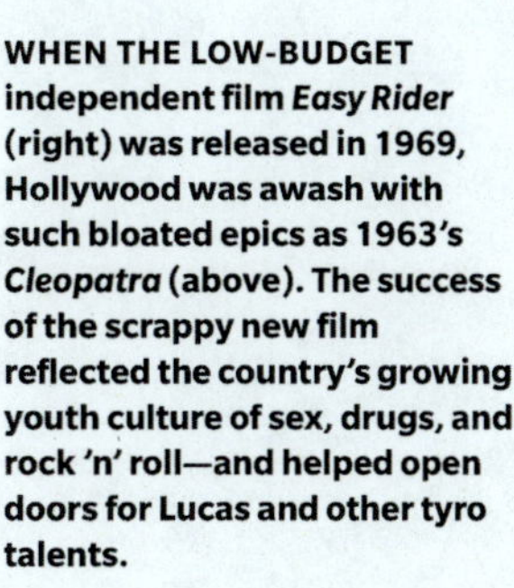

WHEN THE LOW-BUDGET independent film *Easy Rider* (right) was released in 1969, Hollywood was awash with such bloated epics as 1963's *Cleopatra* (above). The success of the scrappy new film reflected the country's growing youth culture of sex, drugs, and rock 'n' roll—and helped open doors for Lucas and other tyro talents.

LUCAS AND HIS FRIEND AND mentor Coppola on the set of Lucas's first feature, 1971's *THX 1138*, based on a short that Lucas had made in school. In *Star Wars*, the film is slyly referenced when Luke Skywalker and Han Solo are moving Chewbacca from "cell block 1138."

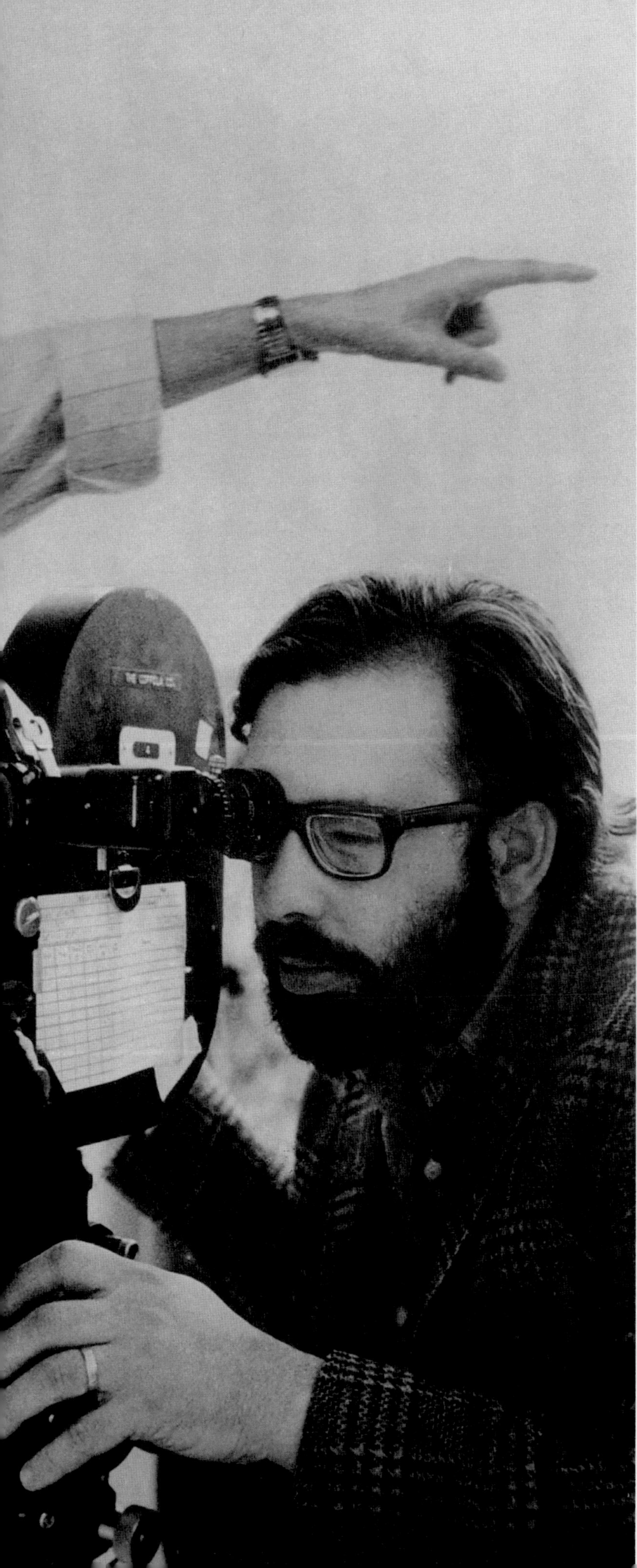

avoid a similar fate, Lucas decided to maintain control over his work by creating Lucasfilm Ltd. Now one of the world's most valuable companies, it had its humble beginnings in Lucas's Mill Valley home, its sole employees George and Marcia Lucas.

Meanwhile, Coppola desperately need money. With the future of American Zoetrope (and his vision of a new Hollywood) at stake, he was forced to take a job directing a mainstream film for Paramount Pictures. "They've just offered me this Italian gangster movie," he told Lucas. "It's like a $3 million potboiler based on a best-seller. Should I do it?"

"I don't think you have a choice," Lucas said.

It was an offer that Coppola couldn't refuse. Reluctantly, he agreed to make *The Godfather.*

On March 11, 1971, *THX 1138* was released to respectful reviews but dismal business. Both Coppola and Marcia thought the film had failed largely because it was cold, humorless, and depressing, reflecting the worst of Lucas's personality traits. "After *THX* went down the toilet, I never said 'I told you so,'" Marcia said, "but I reminded George that I warned him it hadn't involved the audience emotionally."

The criticism rankled Lucas. "Emotionally involving the audience is easy," he said. "Anybody can do it blindfolded. Get a little kitten and have some guy wring its neck." Nevertheless, *THX 1138*'s failure caused him to reevaluate his priorities. "I was working on basically negative movies," he said. "I realized after *THX* that people don't care how the country's being ruined. All that movie did was make people more pessimistic, more depressed, and less willing to get involved in trying to make the world better. We've got to regenerate optimism."

To that end, Lucas started brainstorming ideas with Gary Kurtz, his friend and producer. Initially, they considered remaking Kurosawa's *The Hidden Fortress,* but they were most excited about the idea of making a

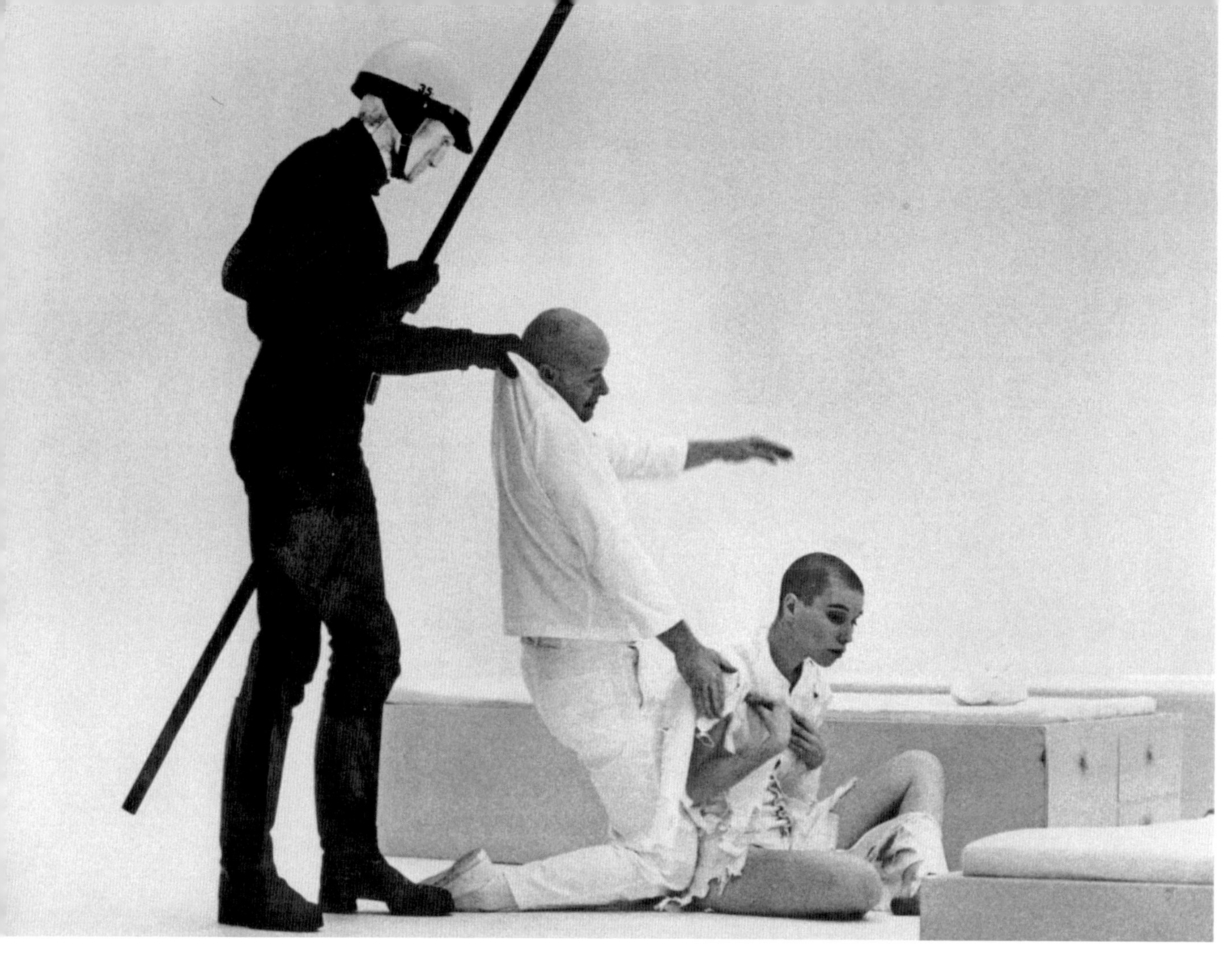

contemporary feature-length version of Lucas's beloved *Flash Gordon.* "I realized that what I really wanted to do was a contemporary action fantasy," Lucas said. It was "something that we wanted to see," Kurtz said, "and no one was making it." Indeed, a sophisticated, contemporary, high-tech, and big-budget version of a children's comic book ("the first multimillion-dollar *Flash Gordon* kind of movie," Lucas said) was virtually unheard of at that time.

In the 1970s, science fiction entered a period of transition, with writers such as Samuel L. Delany and Frank Herbert bringing sophisticated themes and literary experimentation to a genre firmly rooted in pulp. But Lucas's new idea was a deliberate throwback—not truly science fiction so much as fairy tale, fantasy, or "space opera." Lucas himself thought of his *Flash Gordon* film in terms of Arthur Conan Doyle's epigraph to *The Lost World*: "I have wrought my simple plan / If I give one hour of joy / To the boy who's half a man / Or the man who's half a boy."

Unfortunately, the rights to *Flash Gordon* weren't available—King Features Syndicate wanted Federico Fellini to direct the film—so Lucas decided to create his own interstellar hero. "I realized that I could make up a character as easily as [*Flash Gordon* creator] Alex Raymond, whose characters were inspired by Edgar Rice Burroughs," he said. But, in the direct aftermath of *THX 1138,* he wasn't ready to helm another science fiction film. The question was: What next? Coppola provided an answer. "Why don't you try to write something out of your own life that has warmth and humor?" he asked.

Taking his mentor's advice, Lucas remembered nights spent cruising Modesto's main streets, listening to rock 'n' roll and the howls of the deejay Wolfman Jack. ●

ROBERT DUVALL (THX 1138) and Maggie McOmie (LUH 3417) in a scene from *THX 1138* (this page). Opposite: Lucas and a crew member set up a scene with Duvall. Lucas said he wanted the film to be "something that would look like a documentary crew had made a film about some character in a time yet to come."

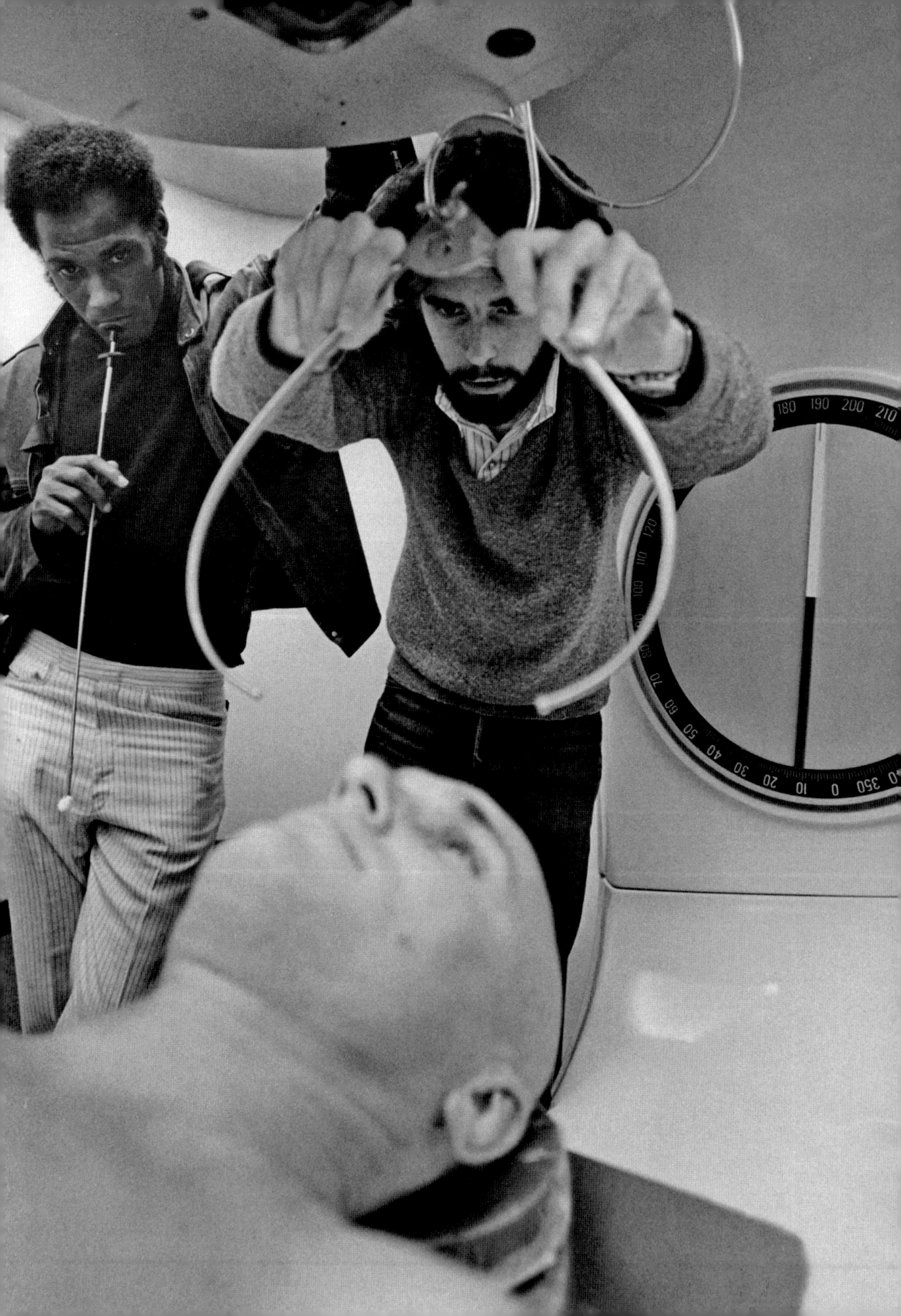
180 190 200 210
120 110 100
70 60 50 40 30 20 10 0 350

Lucas on the San Francisco set of 1973's *American Graffiti*.

CHAPTER 2

An American Auteur

HOW LUCAS'S BIG-BUDGET SCIENCE FICTION PROJECT WAS FUELED BY A FILM ABOUT HIS DRAG-RACING ADOLESCENCE

I N THE YEARS SINCE GEORGE Lucas had left Modesto, its teenage car culture had gradually died out (a casualty of the economic growth that had commercialized its once-quaint streets), but the director felt that his misspent youth had the makings of a great film—one that might even make people laugh and cry. "I'm gonna show you how easy it is," he told Marcia. "I'll make a film that emotionally involves the audience." He called it *American Graffiti.*

The idea proved a hard sell in Hollywood—until *THX 1138* was shown at the prestigious Cannes Film Festival in May 1971. Unable to afford a hotel and lacking festival tickets, Lucas and Marcia had to stay in a campground and sneak into the screening of the film.

The trip paid off when Lucas met with United Artists president David Picker, who offered him $10,000 to develop *American Graffiti.* When Picker asked if he had any other ideas, Lucas told him about his "space opera fantasy film in the vein of *Flash Gordon.*"

"Great," Picker said. "We'll make a deal for that, too."

"And that was really the birth of *Star Wars,*" Lucas later said. "It was only a notion up to then—at that point, it became an obligation."

In addition to *Star Wars,* Lucas was still planning to direct *Apocalypse Now,* but first he had to finish *American Graffiti.* Hoping to avoid writing the script, he used Picker's development budget to hire an outside writer.

LUCAS SET UP A SHOT WITH his crew—including noted cinematographer Haskell Wexler (far right). "There were considerable logistical problems with the cars, cold weather, arguments, all aggravated by the lack of sleep," said producer Gary Kurtz of the film's 28-day Northern California shoot.

SC

Unhappy with the results but fresh out of money, Lucas realized that he would have to write *American Graffiti* himself. "I don't have a natural talent for writing," he said. "When I sit down, I bleed on the page, and it's just awful. Writing just doesn't flow in a creative surge the way other things do." In the end, Picker rejected Lucas's script—partly because it relied too heavily on a rock 'n' roll soundtrack, an unprecedented idea that would cost a small fortune in licensing fees. (Lucas called the film "a musical.") Not least, the youth-movie vogue launched by *Easy Rider* had ended in the early '70s—symbolically, if nothing else—with the failure of Hopper's incomprehensible second film, *The Last Movie.*

Picker's rejection devastated Lucas, who worried that he would never work in Hollywood again. "The easiest job you'll ever get is to try to make your first film," he said, "because nobody knows whether you can make a film or not . . . After you've done that feature, then you have a heck of a difficult time getting your second film off the ground. They look at your first film and they say, 'Oh, well we don't want you anymore.'"

To be fair, Lucas was offered directing jobs—including *Lady Ice,* a caper film starring Donald Sutherland, and movie versions of the Who's rock opera *Tommy* and the Broadway musical *Hair,* but he held out for *American Graffiti.* "That was a very dark period for me," he said. "I was in debt to my parents, in debt to Francis Coppola, in debt to my agent; I was so far in debt I thought I'd never get out." Living on the meager money that Marcia was earning by editing Michael Ritchie's 1972 film, *The Candidate,* Lucas was barely getting by: "Writing, struggling, with no money in the bank . . . getting little jobs, eking out a living," he said. "Trying to stay alive, and pushing a script that nobody wanted."

His determination paid off in early 1972. Universal's Ned Tanen agreed to make *American Graffiti* on the condition that it feature a bona fide star—an expensive proposition, given that the soundtrack would eat up a good chunk

RICHARD DREYFUSS (LEFT) was one of several little-known actors who found stardom after *American Graffiti* became a breakout hit. Above: A rehearsal for the film's sock hop sequence, which was choreographed by Toni Basil, who later became a pop star and had the hit "Mickey" in 1982.

of the film's initial $750,000 budget. In the end, instead of a star actor, Tanen settled for a star producer: Francis Ford Coppola.

Though Coppola hadn't wanted to direct *The Godfather* and had struggled throughout the punishing shoot ("It was just nonstop anxiety," the director said), the film proved an artistic and commercial triumph when it was released in March 1972. Overnight, Coppola became the toast of Hollywood.

With his star producer on board, Lucas spent five months assembling a cast of unknowns who would go on to become some of the decade's biggest celebrities—including Ron Howard, Cindy Williams, Mackenzie Phillips, Richard Dreyfuss, and Suzanne Somers. Perhaps the most significant addition was Harrison Ford, an out-of-work actor who moonlighted as a carpenter. Though he would eventually become a Lucas stalwart and a major star, Ford balked when he learned he would earn only $480 a week—the Screen Actors Guild minimum. "I'm already making $1,000 a week as a carpenter, and I have a young family to support," he told Lucas. After the director agreed to raise his rate to $500, Ford accepted.

Partly inspired by Fellini's 1953 coming-of-age film, *I Vitelloni, American Graffiti* focuses on four young men during a single night in Modesto at the end of the summer of 1962. Heading to college, Steve (Howard) loans his car to the awkward Terry (Charles Martin Smith), giving the boy the confidence to woo Debbie (Candy Clark). Despite an academic scholarship, Curt (Dreyfuss) isn't sure he wants to leave town—especially

ABOVE: CANDY CLARK, Charles Martin Smith, and Ron Howard in *American Graffiti*. Opposite: Lucas on the set with cast and crew. The 1932 Ford deuce coupe became the film's most iconic car and one of several souped-up race cars featured in Lucas's movie. Its license plate number, THX 138, makes a wink to his previous film.

after a mysterious blonde in a Thunderbird (Somers) flirts with him. Challenged by outsider Bob Falfa (Ford), John (Paul Le Mat) struggles to retain his status as the town's leading hot-rodder. Throughout the film, the boys' dreams and desires—and what little exists of the plot—are driven (quite literally) by cars.

On June 26, filming began in San Rafael, California, for *American Graffiti*—a brutal 28-day shoot that took place entirely at night. "It was a very, very, very fast and short schedule, especially considering it was all on location with cars that broke down and all the other drama that would go on," said Lucas. "We had focus problems on the camera, and the assistant cameraman was run over by a car. Then we had a five-alarm fire. That was a typical night." And then the cast and crew had to relocate to Petaluma after San Rafael businesses complained about the streets that were closed to accommodate the shoot.

Some of the drama stemmed from the antics of the youthful cast. "If you put a group of young people in a Holiday Inn, what's going to happen?" asked Clark. "There's going to be some drinking." One of the worst offenders was Ford, who—fueled by the beer he guzzled—climbed the Holiday Inn sign and threw empty bottles into the hotel parking lot. Eventually, his behavior got so bad that producer Gary Kurtz had to reprimand him: "No more drinking beer on the streets, and then no more drinking beer in the trailer, and then no more drinking beer," Ford said.

Coping with *American Graffiti*'s logistics exhausted Lucas, who didn't like directing any more than he liked writing. It also exacerbated the symptoms of his diabetes, which he'd been diagnosed with after graduating from USC. "It's excruciating," he said of completing the shoot. "It's horrible. You get physically sick. I get a very bad cough and a cold whenever I direct." In the end, what Lucas loved best was editing: "That's when I'm going to make my choices," he told Howard.

Since *American Graffiti*'s editor, Verna Fields, was simultaneously editing Peter Bogdanovich's *Paper Moon,* she delegated much of the work to her assistant, Marcia Lucas—a fact that gave George more control than he would otherwise have had. The process also gave him a future character name: Sound editor Walter Murch referred to one of the film's elements, "reel 2, dialogue 2," as "R2-D2." Lucas liked how R2-D2 sounded and made a note of it.

On January 28, 1973, the first public screening of *American Graffiti* was held at San Francisco's Northpoint Theater. Lucas and Coppola were in the audience. So were Tanen and other Universal suits, who had pinned their box office hopes on *Jesus Christ Superstar,* the film version of the popular Andrew Lloyd Webber–Tim Rice rock opera. "*American Graffiti* was an afterthought," Lucas's USC friend Matthew Robbins said. "In some circles at the studio it was, I think, considered a mistake." But the San Francisco audience applauded as soon as "Rock Around the Clock" began playing over the opening credits, and their enthusiasm intensified as the film unfolded. "It was a fabulous screening," Howard said.

Lucas and Coppola were thrilled—until they ran into Tanen. "This film is not ready to be shown to an

LUCAS AND FRANCIS COPPOLA in 1975 in San Francisco, where the filmmakers set up their company, American Zoetrope. "We came to San Francisco because we could," said sound editor Walter Murch, "but also because we had a dream, maybe illusory, that we could make films anywhere."

"I NEEDED A JOB VERY BADLY. I DIDN'T KNOW WHAT WAS GOING TO HAPPEN WITH *GRAFFITI*."

—GEORGE LUCAS

audience," said the furious executive, who had decided to trim the film without Lucas's input. The studio even wanted a new title, suggesting such names as *Another Slow Night in Modesto, Goodbye Burger City, Make Out at Burger City,* and *Wake Me Up, I'm Getting Older.*

An enraged Lucas vowed never to relinquish control to Hollywood executives again. "They're people who have never made a movie in their lives—agents and lawyers with no idea of dramatic flow," he said. "But they can come in, see a movie twice, and in those few hours they can tell you to take this out or shorten that."

With *American Graffiti* in Universal's hands, a weary Lucas started kicking around ideas for *Star Wars,* but since it had been rejected, along with *American Graffiti,* by United Artists, he ultimately turned his focus back to preproduction work on *Apocalypse Now.* "We were all ready to go," Lucas said—Kurtz had gone so far as to scout locations in Hong Kong and the Philippines—but everything fell apart when Coppola refused to cede his percentage of the film's profits (called points) to Columbia. Instead, he suggested that they take part of Lucas's share. "My points were going to shrink way down," Lucas said, "and I wasn't going to do the film for free."

Annoyed, Lucas decided to move on. "I was in debt," he said. "I needed a job very badly. I didn't know what was going to happen with *Graffiti.*" Well, no one did. After it was released on August 1, *American Graffiti* surprised everyone (not least Universal) by becoming an overnight smash. Eventually earning more than $115 million, it turned out to be one of the most profitable films ever made—a success largely driven by nostalgia for a vanished age.

Despite its tagline ("Where were you in '62?"), *American Graffiti* remains indelibly associated with the 1950s—not surprisingly, since the early 1960s practically *were* the 1950s. When American Graffiti was released in the summer of 1973, the film's sock hops, ducktails, and small-town drag races already seemed like relics of a distant past.

In that short time America had been upended. A year after the film takes place, President John F. Kennedy was assassinated, followed by the Beatles' debut on *The Ed Sullivan Show,* the escalation of the Vietnam War, and the Summer of Love. During those same years Martin Luther King Jr. was killed, hippie culture blossomed, and then Woodstock attracted some 500,000 people. By 1973, the United States had only just withdrawn its troops from Southeast Asia and the nation was in the midst of the national nightmare of the Watergate scandal that ended Richard Nixon's presidency. "*Graffiti* is about the fact that you have to accept these changes—they were on the horizon—and if you didn't, you had problems," Lucas said. "You try to fight it . . . and you lose."

Thanks to his new film's success, Lucas had become an A-list director who could seemingly make any film he wanted to. No longer involved with *Apocalypse Now,* he wanted to make *Star Wars.* There was only one problem: No one else did. ●

CHAPTER 3

Star Wars Is Born

HOW THE WRITING AND CASTING OF LUCAS'S "*FLASH GORDON* KIND OF MOVIE" BEDEVILED THE EMBATTLED DIRECTOR

STAR WARS WAS PARTLY A reaction to the presidency of Richard Nixon. "It was really about the Vietnam War, and that was the period where Nixon was trying to run for a [second] term, which got me to thinking historically about how do democracies get turned into dictatorships?" Lucas said. "Because the democracies aren't overthrown; they're given away."

FIRE SALE

THE STORY OF LUKE Skywalker—a humble farm boy who rescues Princess Leia from the clutches of Darth Vader and saves the heroic Rebel Alliance by blowing up the evil Empire's Death Star—has become something of a modern myth and an astronomically profitable franchise. But after United Artists and David Picker rejected *Star Wars,* the only Hollywood executive to take an interest in the film was Alan Ladd Jr., 20th Century Fox's vice president for creative affairs, who met with Lucas just before the release of *American Graffiti.*

Even Ladd was on the fence about *Star Wars,* but he was impressed by Lucas himself—especially after viewing *American Graffiti.* "It absolutely bowled me over," said Ladd, who offered Lucas $15,000 to develop the movie then called *The Star Wars,* $150,000 to write and direct, a $3 million budget, and a $10,000 signing

THE LOVE TRIANGLE AT THE heart of *Star Wars* was mirrored in real life. Mark Hamill, left, was smitten with Carrie Fisher, who had a three-month affair with Harrison Ford, a married father of two. "It was so intense," the actress later said. "It was Han and Leia during the week, and Carrie and Harrison during the weekend."

IN A 1976 LETTER TO A FRIEND, Alec Guinness wrote of working with the *Star Wars* cast, calling Ford "Tennyson . . . a rangy, languid young man who is probably intelligent and amusing. But Oh God, God, they make me feel ninety—and treat me as if I was 106."

bonus. When *American Graffiti* became an established hit, agent Jeff Berg told Lucas that he should demand more money to direct *The Star Wars*: He was now "a $500,000 director," the agent said. Lucas demurred. "I don't want to be a $500,000 director," he said. "I will write and direct the movie for the price I agreed to write and direct the movie."

He did, however, demand the rights to make the sequels and to retain the merchandising profits. "I simply said, 'I'm gonna be able to make T-shirts, I'm gonna be able to make posters, and I'm gonna be able to sell this movie even though the studio won't,'" Lucas said. Since merchandising was then considered a disposable afterthought, Fox gave Lucas what he wanted—a concession that eventually cost the studio many millions of dollars. "George was enormously farsighted, and the studio wasn't, because they didn't know the world was changing," one Fox executive later said. "George *did* know the world was changing. I mean, *he changed it.*"

Though Lucas had been paid a mere $65,000 for *American Graffiti*, his percentage of the gross had made him a millionaire. The money allowed him to invest in real estate—including a house in San Anselmo that he called Parkhouse—but success brought what he called "an infinite number of distractions." Not least, Lucas found it increasingly difficult to finish the first draft of his science fiction script, which was due on October 31, 1973, just two months after *American Graffiti* came out. That was a deadline Lucas would not meet.

Part of the problem was Lucas's unbridled ambition. Though *Star Wars* had its origins in pure pulp, from the beginning Lucas saw his film as far more than a genre throwback. "The original inspiration for *Star Wars* was to try to create a modern myth," he said. "Westerns were the last mythological genre we had, but they had died out in the late 1950s, early 1960s, and nothing had replaced them."

Much has been made of *Star Wars'* debt to the work of Joseph Campbell, the American scholar whose 1949 book, *The Hero with a Thousand Faces,* posits the existence of a "monomyth," a universal story known as "the hero's journey" that mirrors human development from childhood to maturity. Essentially, Campbell suggests, all epic heroes—Osiris, Prometheus, Moses, and Jesus among them—experience a journey that involves three major stages: departure, initiation, and return. The concept showed Lucas how to approach his modern fairy tale. "I began to understand how I could do this," he said. "It was a great gift."

But Campbell was only one of many influences on the developing film. Over time, the genre tropes of *Flash Gordon* and Edgar Rice Burroughs were augmented by the sophisticated science fiction of Frank Herbert's 1965 novel, *Dune,* which featured elements that were reflected in *Star Wars*—including a mystical sect and a ruthless emperor.

Cinematically, Akira Kurosawa's *The Hidden Fortress* and *Seven Samurai* were hugely important to Lucas, as were World War II documentaries and children's fantasy films. "I researched kids' movies and how they work and how myths work, and I looked very

ACTORS KENNY BAKER (R2-D2) and Anthony Daniels (C-3PO) in Watford, England (above, left). At right: The actors in costume in Tunisia. "The truth is that the robots didn't work at all," Lucas said. "Threepio works very painfully . . . I couldn't get Artoo to go more than a few feet without running into something."

"*STAR WARS* IS A CLASSIC STORY, AN OLD-STYLE NARRATIVE, EVEN BLATANTLY OLD-FASHIONED."
—GEORGE LUCAS

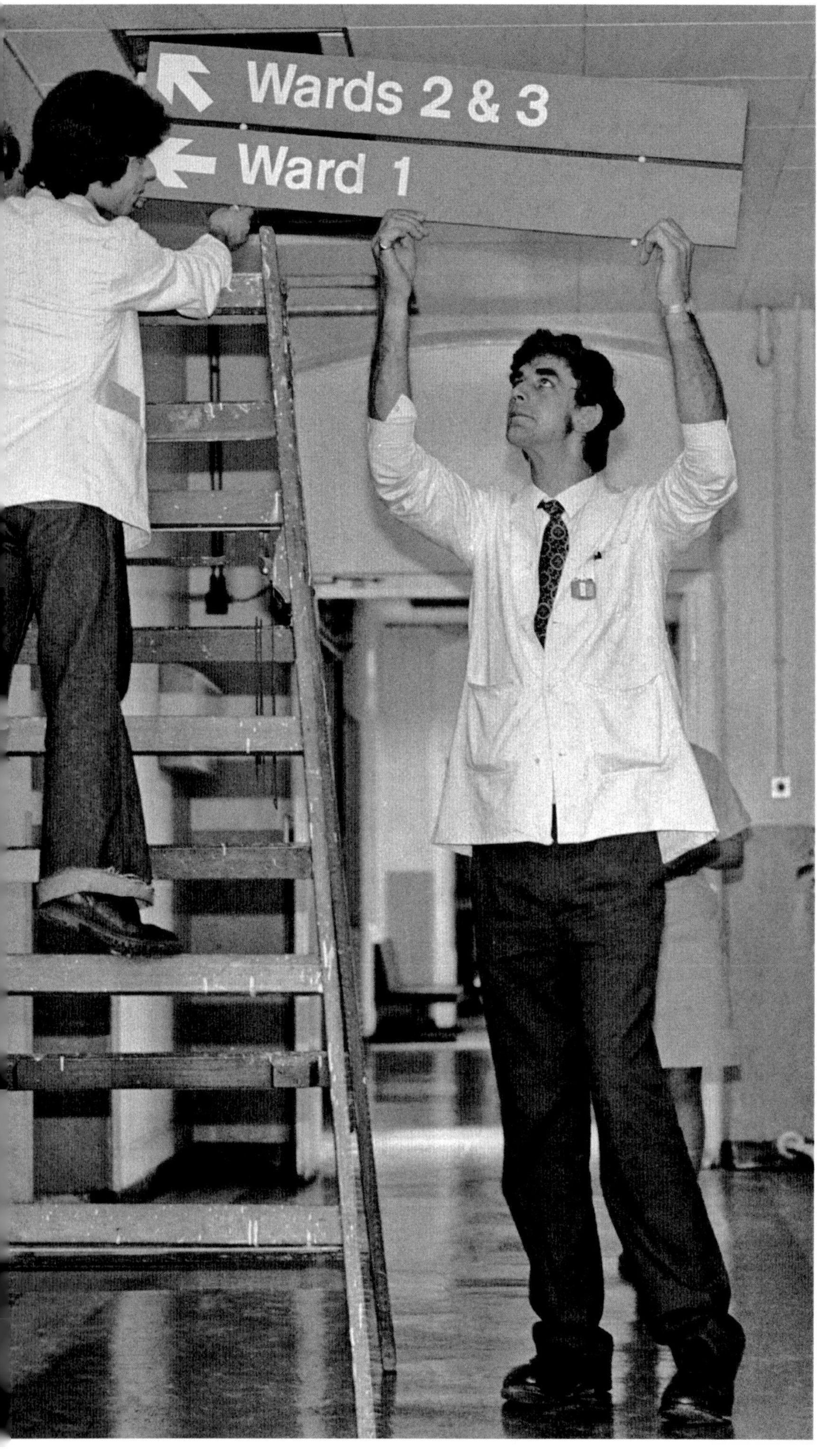

PETER MAYHEW, WHO WAS seven foot three, was working at a London hospital (above) when he was cast as Chewbacca, Han Solo's copilot (opposite). "He was the closest any human being could be to a Wookiee," said Lucas after the actor died in 2019: "Big heart, gentle nature."

carefully at the elements of films within that fairy tale genre which made them successful," Lucas said. "I found that they always took place over the hill, in some exotic, far-off land. For the Greeks, it was Ulysses going off into the unknown. For America, it was out west... the last place left 'over the hill' is space."

The Vietnam War was another influence on *Star Wars*—thanks to Lucas's work on *Apocalypse Now.* "I was interested in the human side of the war and the fact that here was a great nation with all this technology which was losing a war to basically tribesmen," Lucas said—a conflict that would eventually be reflected by *Star Wars'* fight between the Empire and the Rebel Alliance.

Seemingly insignificant moments from Lucas's life made their way into the movie, as well. One day, as he watched Marcia driving with their massive Alaskan malamute, Indiana, in the passenger seat, Lucas thought it looked like the dog was her copilot—an idea that inspired the creation of Han Solo's copilot, the Wookiee Chewbacca. (Lucas later gave the dog's name to the hero of 1981's *Raiders of the Lost Ark.*)

Lucas had begun writing in early 1973 by jotting down the names of possible characters—including Emperor Ford Xerxes II, Biggs, Owen, Valorum, and (yes) Luke Skywalker. Titled *The Journal of the Whills,* the narrative began: "This is the story of Mace Windy, a revered Jedi-bendu of Opuchi, as related to us by C.J. Thorpe, padawan learner to the famed Jedi." After writing that his heroes were "summoned to the desolate second planet of Yoshiro by a mysterious courier from the Chairman of the alliance," Lucas simply stopped, having presumably run out of inspiration.

Not long afterward, Lucas began a second draft that emphasized elements that would be part of the finished film—including a hero named Luke Skywalker, a "laser sword," a cantina sequence, a dogfight in space, a captive

princess, and an awards ceremony.

Lucas delivered his rough draft in the spring of 1974—nearly eight months after the October 1973 deadline. Though unformed and often incomprehensible, this version contained the bare bones of the final film: two bickering comic droids, Han Solo (at that point conceived of as an alien monster), Princess Leia, Wookiees, and an evil general named Darth Vader. Most important, it featured the first mention of the Force, then known as "the Force of Others."

The concept of the Force, more than any other element, is arguably most responsible for *Star Wars'* enduring success. "The Force is really a way of seeing," Lucas later said. "It's a way of being with life." It also reflected existential issues that had preoccupied Lucas since childhood. "When I was 10 years old, I asked my mother . . . 'If there's only one God, why are there so many religions?'" he said. "And over the years—I've been pondering that question ever since. And it would seem to me that the conclusion that I've come to is that all the religions are true, they just see a different part of the elephant. A religion is basically a container for faith. Faith is the glue that holds us together as a society. Faith in our culture . . . is a very important part

GIVEN A CHOICE BETWEEN playing Chewbacca or Darth Vader, the six-foot-seven English bodybuilder David Prowse (opposite, in 1972's *Vampire Circus*) chose the villain, because he didn't want to be invisible in an animal suit. It wasn't until his first costume fitting that he learned he would be just as anonymous playing Vader (this page).

"THE FORCE IS REALLY A WAY OF SEEING. IT'S A WAY OF BEING WITH LIFE."

—GEORGE LUCAS

of, I think, allowing us to remain stable, remain balanced." *Star Wars,* Lucas said, takes "all the issues that religion represents and [tries] to distill them down into a more modern, more easily accessible construct that people can grab onto to accept the fact that there is a greater mystery out there."

By January 1975, Lucas finished a second draft of his script, now called *Adventures of the Starkiller: Episode I: The Star Wars,* which was more focused than the previous versions. "The story was too big for one movie," he said. "I had $3 million, and I thought, 'No way—I have got to cut this down.' So I broke it down, making the first act as the first film and putting the second and third acts on the shelf to film later. It was the only way I could carry on with the script." Still, even that "first act" remained overburdened with characters and ideas. "Anybody who read those drafts said, 'What are you doing here?'" producer Gary Kurtz said. "'This is absolute gobbledygook.'"

Lucas soldiered on. In August, he finished a third draft, the first to feature a character explicitly inspired by Carlos Castaneda's 1968 book, *The Teachings of Don Juan: A Yaqui Way of Knowledge.* "Old man can do magic, read minds, talk to things like Don

LUCAS INSPECTED A MODEL **of the Death Star (above), the site of the space dogfight he imagined as an "aerial ballet." Opposite: World War II movies, such as 1954's *The Bridges at Toko-Ri* (top), influenced *Star Wars'* battles (bottom).**

"HELP ME, OBI-WAN KENOBI. You're my only hope!" Leia programs R2-D2 with a message for the Jedi Master. He "wanted me to be proud and frightening," Fisher said of Lucas's view of her role. "I was not a damsel in distress. I was a distressing damsel."

Juan," Lucas wrote. His name was General Ben Kenobi.

That same month, Lucas began casting the film. The biggest challenge involved the chemistry between Luke Skywalker, Princess Leia, and Han Solo. He had to get that right. (The name "Skywalker," incidentally, had overtaken Lucas's initial idea of "Starkiller." After the Charles Manson murders in Hollywood, Lucas didn't want any unseemly connotations.) By December, having briefly considered casting Robby Benson as Skywalker and Jodie Foster as Leia (both of whom were rising stars), Lucas had narrowed his choices down to two potential trios: The first, intense and serious, was composed of Will Seltzer as Luke, 16-year-old Terri Nunn as Leia, and an odd, slightly sinister New York actor named Christopher Walken as Han. The second trio, more goofy and lighthearted, consisted of Mark Hamill, Carrie Fisher, and Harrison Ford. (For her part, Fisher accepted happily despite the condition that she lose 10 pounds. She was enthusiastic about the film, later saying—perhaps looking forward to dining in the studio commissary—"I wanted to have lunch with monsters.")

Fox exec Ladd, though, was "very nervous" about the cast of unknowns—a reticence that was only slightly tempered by the fact that Sir Alec Guinness had agreed to play Obi-Wan Kenobi. The great British actor was in Los Angeles filming Neil Simon's 1976 movie *Murder by Death* when he was given the script. Guinness was no fan of science fiction—he initially dismissed the script as "fairy tale rubbish"—but he knew that the director, whom he called "Paul Lucas," had directed *American Graffiti.* He also needed money to produce a play in London. In the end, he agreed to do the film in exchange for both a salary and profit points—a decision that would make him a very wealthy man.

With casting completed, Lucas began overseeing the visuals and sound, location scouting, and other

preproduction logistics. The biggest challenge involved creating the complex special effects Lucas had envisioned, which involved an entirely new conception of space, with, for example, spaceships being able to move in the way that fighter planes did in movie dogfights. "I'd seen [spaceships] flying around in serials like *Flash Gordon,* but they were really dopey," he said. "And in *2001,* it was slow. Very, very brilliant, but not what I was interested in. I wanted to see this incredible aerial ballet in outer space."

To illustrate what he wanted, Lucas showed his special-effects wizard, John Dykstra, a reel of dogfights he had cut together from World War II films. There was only one problem: The technology Lucas needed to deliver these effects didn't exist. That didn't deter Lucas, who simply created his own special-effects company, Industrial Light & Magic (ILM), to facilitate his vision, while Dykstra invented a new camera, the "Dykstraflex."

In January 1976, Lucas finished his fourth—and final—draft of *The Star Wars.* (The "The" was dropped during production.) Though the script had been considerably improved by eliminating much of the exposition that had weighted down earlier drafts, Lucas remained unsatisfied. "I had a lot of vague concepts, but I didn't really know where to go with it, and I've never fully resolved it," he said. "I'm still not very happy with the script. I never have been."

On March 22, 1976, *Star Wars* began filming in Tunisia—and that's when the *real* troubles began. ●

ONE OF THE TUSKEN RAIDERS who menace Skywalker on Tatooine (above); Greedo, the Rodian bounty hunter that Han shoots in Mos Eisley (opposite, top); and Doug Beswick, part of the team of artists who created these Bith musicians for Figrin D'an and the Modal Nodes, the band that plays in the Mos Eisley cantina (bottom).

CHAPTER 4

The "Impossible" Dream

HOW ENDLESS SETBACKS MADE LUCAS'S RISKY NEW FILM LOOK LIKE A CERTAIN DISASTER

GEORGE LUCAS AND ANTHONY Daniels (C-3PO) on the set of the Lars moisture farm homestead on Tatooine, where Luke grew up.

LOCATED IN THE CENTER OF Africa's north coast, Tunisia was chosen to stand in for Tatooine, Luke Skywalker's humble desert home. The filming conditions seemed ideal—the country hadn't seen rain for seven years. That changed as soon as *Star Wars* started shooting in March of 1976. "We went at the wrong time," said Gil Taylor, the film's director of photography. "Instead of getting hard sun, we got terrible weather . . . we had rain for four days."

That was only the start of the troubles. As Lucas shot his first scene (Luke and his uncle Owen purchasing C-3PO and R2-D2), the electronic droid that was R2-D2 didn't work well. Meanwhile Anthony Daniels, the live actor who played C-3PO, struggled inside his unwieldy costume. "I felt like I was being stabbed with a pair of scissors every time I made a gesture," he said.

During the two weeks of shooting in the desert, a storm destroyed sets; robots

MARK HAMILL, KENNY BAKER, Daniels, and Alec Guinness clowned in the Tunisian desert, belying the discomfort almost everyone felt on the troublesome set. The film's production designer, John Barry, first used the remote location for director Stanley Donen's 1974 film adaptation of Antoine de Saint-Exupéry's *The Little Prince*.

consistently malfunctioned; and local food gave everyone stomach problems. "There were nothing but stumbling blocks," said J.W. Rinzler, author of *The Making of Star Wars*. "All through shooting Lucas had problems." In the end, Lucas captured only about half of what he'd envisioned. "I thought the film was in trouble," he said. By his own admission, part of the problem was his inexperience. "I made this movie by the seat of my pants," he later said. "I didn't really know what I was doing."

He knew what he *wanted,* however. Though science fiction films had traditionally been defined by a pristine quality, Lucas envisioned what he called a "used universe," according to Lorne Peterson, a *Star Wars* model maker. "I remember the idea came down from him. And he didn't want anything too slick or too well painted. It needed to look aged and also boilerplate technology. Everything had to look like it had been riveted together, assembled, rather than just this slick mono-shape."

That meant greasy robots, weather-worn buildings, and spaceships that were battered like the cars Lucas had driven as a kid. "The film has to make us believe it really existed, that we've really gone to another galaxy to shoot," he said. "The success of the imaginary, it's to make something totally fabricated seem real." (Gamely, Guinness rolled in the sand to give his costume a weathered look.)

After desert shooting wrapped, *Star Wars* began filming at London's Elstree Studios on April 7. "I was hoping things would go better," Lucas said, "but they didn't." Though it's generally easier to film in controlled studio conditions than on location, that wasn't the case at Elstree. Part of the problem was the British crew. "Every day it was like trying to push a ball up a hill," Lucas said. "The crew saw it as a dopey film made by this American kid. Nobody went any distance to try and help. It was a tough schedule and they didn't really sympathize with my situation." When told to light Chewbacca, for instance, the director of photography said, "Put some more light on the dog, whatever it's called."

In London, Carrie Fisher and Harrison Ford arrived on the set, and

C-3PO, LUKE SKYWALKER, AND Obi-Wan Kenobi watch as R2-D2 projects Princess Leia's hologram message (opposite). This page: On the set in Tunisia. "I was seriously, seriously depressed at that point, because nothing had gone right," Lucas said of the problem-plagued shoot. "Everything was screwed up."

the film's iconic love triangle—what Lucas thought of as *Casablanca* in space—was together for the first time. Never a fan of working with actors, the director was terse to the point of taciturnity, his instructions often limited to "Same thing, only better" and "Faster, more intense!" He said the latter phrase so often that when he lost his voice, Fisher recalled, "we wanted to get him a little board" with the direction written on it. ("I have a sneaking suspicion that if there were a way to make movies without actors, George would do it," Mark Hamill said.)

Though Lucas was grateful for his relatively trouble-free cast ("Life is too short for crazy actors," he said), drama was brewing behind the scenes. The 19-year-old Fisher was developing a drug habit, for one thing, and she swiftly fell for Ford, who was 14 years her senior and married with children. In her 2016 book, *The Princess Diarist,* the actress recalled how they began an affair that would torment her. "If I'd never succeeded in coaxing this coveted laughter of his out into the waiting world," Fisher wrote, "I would never have known what I was missing—just that I was missing something, besides his not being single or accessible or, for the most part, warm. I wouldn't have been able to imagine his laughing wholeheartedly, or known how amazing it felt to actually be with the person you were with *and* feel that he liked you!"

Despite the teenage angst, Fisher

was nobody's fool, calling herself "the only girl in this sort of adolescent boy's fantasy" and asking, "How about a big cooking scene, baking some space food, or how about me sewing my costume back together? A shopping scene, maybe, on a mall planet. Give me a girlfriend and we'll talk about how cute Han is."

Once again, directing pressures made Lucas sick. "You know you're not going to get 100 percent," he told Marcia Lucas, who traveled to England to cheer him up, "but you think maybe you'll get 70 percent or 80 percent. I'm getting 40 percent every day." He wasn't alone in his concern. Unhappy with the *Star Wars* dailies and alarmed by Lucas's lack of progress, 20th Century Fox threatened to shut the film down.

Part of the problem stemmed from the fact that the special effects weren't finished, though Lucas used some of Industrial Light & Magic's early models to sway skeptical executives. "They were used with George to go to the studios

A STORMTROOPER RIDES A dewback. While there were dewbacks in the original film, Lucas was limited to what he could do because of technical and budgetary limitations. The filmmaker added this reptilian creature along with other elements in the digitally altered 1997 version of *Star Wars*, spurring the ire of many die-hard fans.

to have something visual to talk about," Peterson explained. "To say, 'Well, there will be an X-wing, and it will have a fight and battle with this and this will be the Death Star' and all that kind of stuff . . . to somehow convince studios that this is a reasonable idea."

Even as filming continued in London, the models remained a work in progress back in the States. "There was a mad rush. We had to get this thing done in like a few weeks, so that we wouldn't keep these people waiting in England," said model maker Steve Gawley of the *Millennium Falcon*. "And we had everybody . . . the camera guys dropped their work, they were making parts, and then they brought it to us, and we just put stuff on it. That ship was built really, really quickly and became iconic. Who would have known?" (At one point, someone dropped an early version of the Death Star and dumped the damaged model into the trash, according to Peterson. It later ended up in the hands of a Star Wars memorabilia collector and was exhibited at Seattle's EMP Museum.)

The optical effects were even more problematic—partly because ILM was doing something that had never been done before. After returning to the United States, Lucas discovered that John Dykstra's work was hopelessly stalled. Though he had spent half of ILM's budget, Dykstra had finished only one of the film's more than 360 special-effects shots. Alarmed, Lucas was hospitalized with chest pains. After leaving the hospital the next morning, he took control of ILM and instituted a rigorous new schedule. "Making a movie," Lucas said, "is a terribly painful experience."

He was particularly upset that directing demands forced him to entrust the editing to John Jympson, a Brit who had worked on 1964's *A Hard Day's Night*. Though Lucas had hoped that Jympson would bring some of that film's brisk pace to *Star Wars*, he was unhappy with the results. "I tried to get the editor to cut it my way and he didn't really want to," said Lucas. He

"FASTER, MORE INTENSE!" Lucas kept telling his stars. But the pacing of the scenes was only part of *Star Wars'* frenetic clip. "When it was first released, people thought *Star Wars* moved very, very fast," he said. "Part of that is that you're introduced to a world you've never seen before."

"I EXPECT IT WILL ALL FALL APART NEXT WEEK."

—GEORGE LUCAS ON THE FILM'S INITIAL SUCCESS

THE DEATH OF OBI-WAN Kenobi wasn't part of the original script and was added during filming. Though Lucas said that Guinness was unhappy with the news, the actor claimed that it was his idea. "I just couldn't go on speaking those bloody awful, banal lines," he said. "I'd had enough of the mumbo jumbo."

fired Jympson after finishing work in England. "I had no editor. I was behind schedule, and I had to race to finish the movie."

Working with Marcia, Lucas spent nearly four months editing the attack on the Death Star, the film's climactic sequence, which Fox, in its infinite wisdom, wanted to cut entirely. In the weeks leading up to the *Star Wars* premiere, Fisher visited Lucas while he was editing. "George was lying on the couch, and he'd been up for something like 36 hours," she said. "They were threatening to take the film out of his hands, cut the negative and go right to the theaters. And he looked up at me and said, 'I don't ever want to do this again.'" As Lucas himself told the *New York Times,* "I really want to retire and do a lot of experimental work with film that will probably never be seen by anybody."

Meanwhile, the film was $2 million over its revised $5.25 million budget. "*Star Wars* gained a rather ominous reputation within the studio because the costs were exceeding what had originally been estimated," said one Fox executive. On the heels of the February 1977 screening in Lucas's home for his friends, *Star Wars* was shown to the studio's board of directors. Once again, it was a disaster. "In the end, the lights came up and they walked out," said Gary Kurtz. "There was no reaction at all. We looked at each other and said, 'Uh-oh.'"

The film's problems began with the clunky, overly expository opening crawl, which Brian De Palma—despite his dislike of the film—offered to rewrite. Lucas agreed. Later, Fox would suggest having a narrator recite the words. Lucas refused. "They're going to have to learn to read sooner or later," he joked. "Maybe *Star Wars* will give them an incentive. Maybe we have a valuable tool here. Maybe a whole generation will learn to read just so they can figure out what's going on in *Star Wars.*"

The addition of music helped immeasurably. To score the film,

Steven Spielberg had recommended John Williams, who had composed the distinctive Academy Award–winning score for *Jaws* and was working on Spielberg's new film, *Close Encounters of the Third Kind.* "Do a score like Wagner," Lucas told him. In the end, Williams's music perfectly matched the film's old-fashioned narrative, giving it an added sense of exhilaration and triumph—the antithesis of the spare, electronic scores that were traditionally associated with science fiction films. Lucas was so thrilled with the result that he played part of it over the phone to Spielberg, who worried that Williams might not come up with anything as good for *Close Encounters.*

With its music and special effects finally in place, *Star Wars* premiered at San Francisco's Northpoint Theater on May 1, 1977. A nervous Lucas attended with his colleagues, parents, and wife. "If the audience doesn't cheer when Han Solo comes in at the last second in the *Millennium Falcon* to help Luke when he's being chased by Vader," Marcia told her husband, "the movie doesn't work."

She needn't have worried. The audience started shouting as soon as the first spaceship appeared, and their enthusiasm reached a feverish pitch as the film progressed. When Han came in at the last second to help Luke, they not only cheered—they *exploded.* "I just never had experienced that kind of reaction to any movie *ever,*" said Alan Ladd, who tried to hide his tears of joy by leaving the theater. Outside, George Sr.—the man who'd told his son he would never make a living as an artist—was shaking everyone's hands. "Thank you!" he kept saying. "Thank you very much for helping out George!"

Despite the overwhelmingly positive response, Fox remained skeptical. So did theater owners, who continued to believe that *The Other Side of Midnight* would be one of the summer's big hits and that the science fiction film to beat was *Damnation Alley.* (*Damnation* what?) In contrast, *Star Wars* was slated to open in fewer than

THOUGH *STAR WARS* WAS inspired by the question of why democracies become dictatorships, there is arguably something militaristic about the film. Indeed, the closing ceremony (shown being filmed here) bears more than a passing resemblance to *Triumph of the Will*, Leni Riefenstahl's 1935 documentary about a massive Nazi rally in Nuremberg.

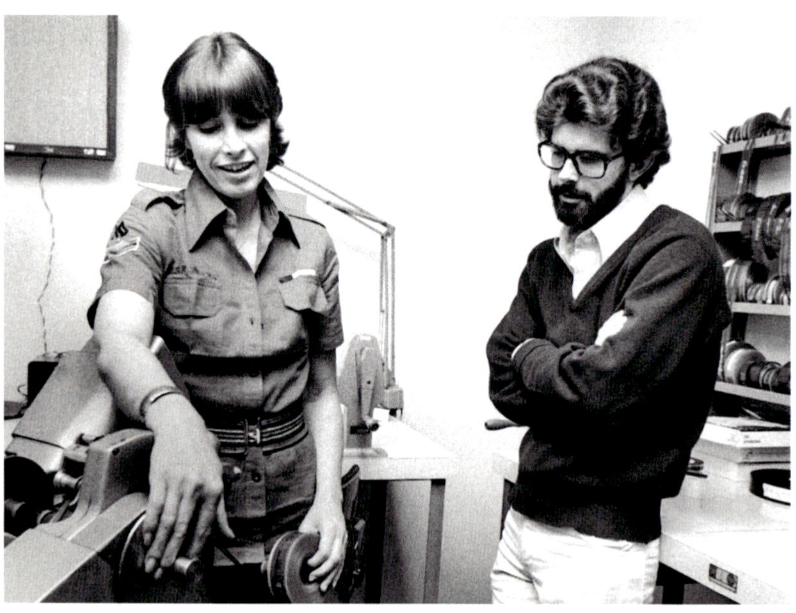

***STAR WARS'* EDITOR, MARCIA** **Lucas (top left), editing the movie with her husband in Los Angeles. Left: One of the film's original posters shows an obvious debt to the science fiction pulp paperbacks that inspired Lucas. Above: Lucas examining footage with his staff.**

"THERE'S A GANG OF PEOPLE OUT THERE WHO DID THIS IMPOSSIBLE STUFF!"

—A HOLLYWOOD INSIDER ON LUCAS AND HIS TEAM

40 theaters nationwide—a ridiculously limited distribution. Even Lucas had low expectations. "I had no idea of what was going to happen," he said. "I mean, I had no idea."

On May 25, the exhausted director was having lunch with Marcia across the street from Mann's Chinese Theatre, where *Star Wars* was beginning its run. (The theater's management had grudgingly booked the film only because *Sorcerer* wasn't finished yet.) "I noticed this huge line that went around the block," Lucas said. "I didn't know what it was."

Even after Lucas learned that they were waiting to see *his* film, he remained wary. A movie's opening weekend isn't necessarily a gauge of its success, especially when it comes to science fiction films, which are traditionally supported by a loyal fan base—at least at first. The true test of a film's popularity, Lucas knew, lies with the general public. "I expect it will all fall apart next week," he said.

It didn't. All across the country, people were lining up before dawn to see *Star Wars*. (In Honolulu, they stood for hours in a tropical storm.) Overwhelmed theater staffs had to turn away thousands of would-be customers, some of whom tried to break down doors in their desperate attempts to see the film. "I've never seen anything like it," one theater manager said. "We're getting all kinds. Old people, young people, children, Hare Krishna groups. They bring cards to play in line. We have checkers players, we have chess players. People with paint and sequins on their faces. Fruit eaters like I've never seen

MANN'S
CHINESE
STAR WARS

before. People loaded on grass and LSD. At least one guy has been here every day. It's an audience participation film. They hiss the villain, they scream and holler and everything else. When school's out, the kids'll go crazy."

They did, along with everyone else, leaving in the lurch theater owners who had bet on *The Other Side of Midnight*—to say nothing of 20th Century Fox executives, who scrambled to expand the film's distribution. By August, *Star Wars* was playing in 800 theaters and gaining critical raves to boot.

Though Lucas had variously called his story a fairy tale, a space opera, and a fantasy, it was, more than anything, a western in outer space. "The sidekicks are salty, squatty robots instead of leathery old cowpokes who scratch their whiskers and say, 'Aw shucks' a lot, and the gunfighters square off with laser swords instead of Colt revolvers," the critic Charles Champlin wrote in the *Los Angeles Times*. "But it is all and gloriously one, the mythic and simple world of the good guys vs. the bad guys . . . the rustlers and the land grabbers, the old generation saving the young with a last heroic gesture, which drives home the message of courage and conviction."

The film's success sent Hollywood into a spin. A group from Disney reportedly came to see the film—"virtually the whole studio," an insider recalled. "They were saying to each other, 'There's a gang of people out there who did this impossible stuff! We've never heard of these guys.'"

When it came to *Star Wars,* Lucas knew, doing the "impossible" had been a scrappy, grueling, seat-of-the-pants process. "And all it took me," he said, "was two years and one garage." ●

"I THINK OF THIS AS A MOVIE Disney would have made when Walt Disney was alive," said Lucas of *Star Wars,* which had its Hollywood premiere at Mann's Chinese Theatre (left). His words proved prescient: In 2012, Lucas sold the Star Wars franchise and Lucasfilm to Disney.

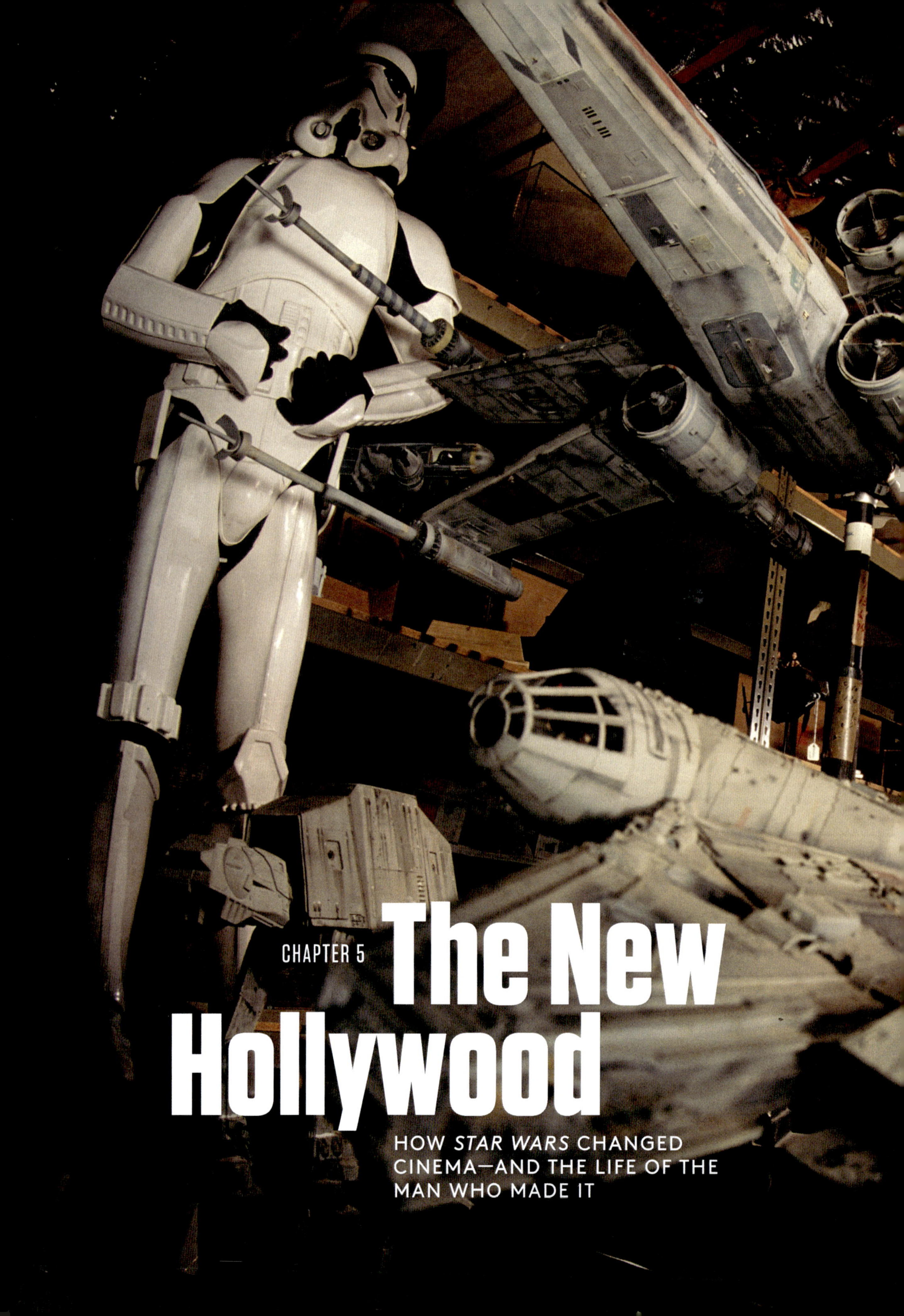

CHAPTER 5

The New Hollywood

HOW *STAR WARS* CHANGED CINEMA—AND THE LIFE OF THE MAN WHO MADE IT

TAKEN IN THE ARCHIVE WAREHOUSE AT Lucas's Skywalker Ranch in Marin County, California, in 1997, this image was commissioned by *Time* magazine because many of the items pictured—including models of the *Millennium Falcon,* the Death Star, and an X-wing fighter—were being donated to the Smithsonian Institution in Washington, D.C.

LUKE SKYWALKER WITH YODA on the swamp-covered planet Dagobah in 1980's *The Empire Strikes Back* (above). The Jedi Master puppet was voiced and operated by Frank Oz, who began his career with Jim Henson's Muppets and later became a successful film director. Opposite: Imperial AT-AT Walkers in the film's Battle of Hoth.

BY 2019, THE FILM THAT Steven Spielberg had predicted would make $100 million had made an astonishing $775 million. In the process, it became a blueprint for the Hollywood blockbuster, which is why it's easy to forget how shockingly innovative it was. In the mid-1970s, innocence and naivete were virtually unheard of in American movies. The film's old-fashioned narrative and cinematic techniques—the opening crawl, the wipes used to transition between scenes, the brassy orchestral score—were so outdated they felt new. Yes, the film borrowed (sometimes slavishly) from a wide variety of sources, but its energy, speed, humor, and optimism were wholly its own. Nevertheless, George Lucas was unsatisfied with the result. "*Star Wars* is about 25 percent of what I wanted it to be," he said. "I think the sequels will be much, much better."

The first one arguably was. Directed by Irvin Kershner, 1980's *The Empire Strikes Back* is widely considered the best of the initial trilogy. "After the space opera cheerfulness of the original film, this one plunges into darkness and even despair, and surrenders more completely to the underlying mystery of the story," critic Roger Ebert wrote. "It is because of the emotions stirred in *Empire* that the entire series takes on a mythic quality."

The following year saw the release of *Raiders of the Lost Ark,* the film that Lucas had conceived while trying to avoid writing *Star Wars.* (After Spielberg told Lucas that he'd always wanted to direct a James Bond movie, Lucas said, "I've got a better film than that. Have you ever heard of the Ark of the Covenant?"")

The third Star Wars film, *Return of the Jedi,* directed by Richard Marquand, with Lucas as co-writer and executive producer, sold a record $6.2 million worth of tickets on its opening day in 1983. After that movie, though, 16 years passed before anything emerged from a galaxy far, far away. "I wasn't interested in doing another frustrating, imagination-inhibiting experience like *Star Wars,* where I was working around the technology and cutting back on the story," Lucas said.

Thanks to Industrial Light & Magic's ongoing innovations, it wasn't long before Lucas had the technology to do what he'd always wanted. The big breakthrough came with the CGI effects that the company created for *Jurassic Park,* Spielberg's 1993 film about dinosaurs run amok. That same year, production began on *Toy Story,* the first completely computer-generated feature film and the first hit from Pixar Animation Studios, which had begun as a division of Lucasfilm. "I

LEIA IS HELD CAPTIVE BY Jabba the Hutt in 1983's *Return of the Jedi,* the third Star Wars film. Director Richard Marquand was, not surprisingly, micromanaged by Lucas on the set. "George harassed Richard Marquand into more or less doing what he wanted," said Gary Kurtz, "and I think the film suffered because of that."

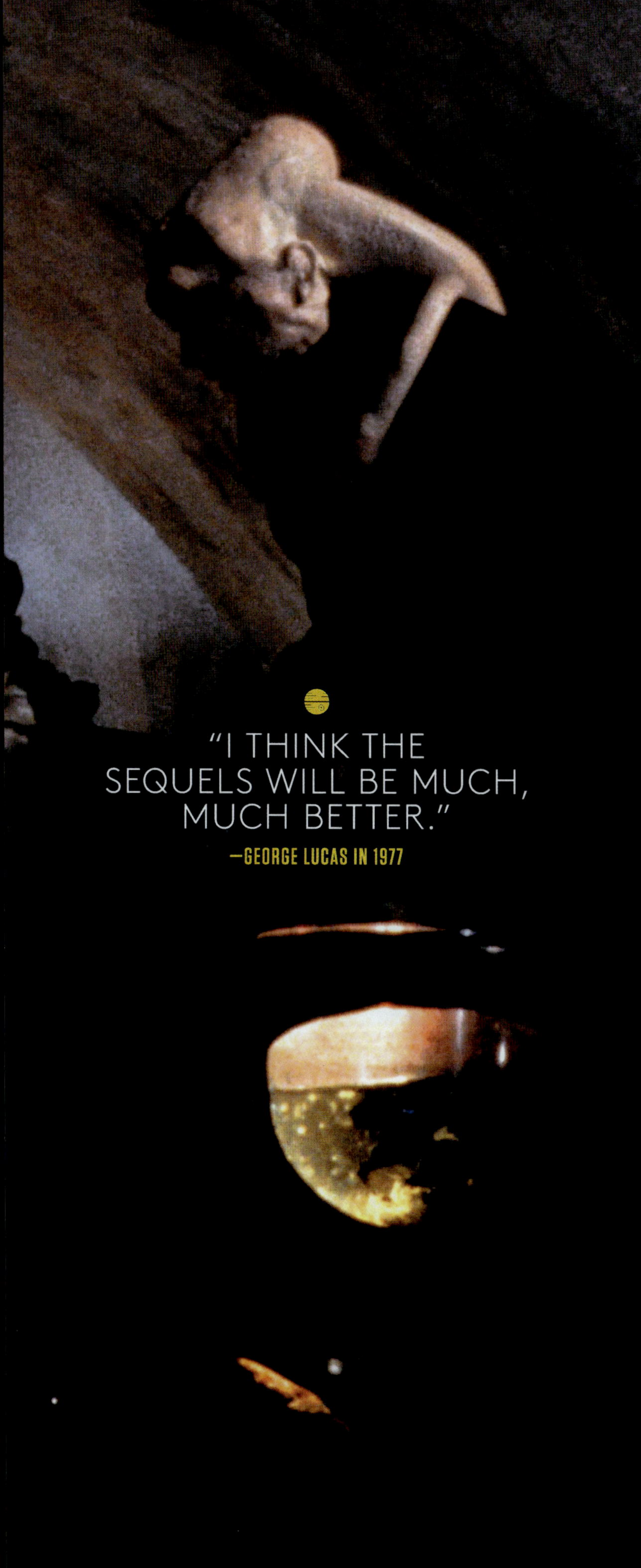

"I THINK THE SEQUELS WILL BE MUCH, MUCH BETTER."

—GEORGE LUCAS IN 1977

think we may have reached a level here where we have actually artificially created reality, which of course is what the movies have been trying to do all along," Lucas said.

Spurred by his company's advances, Lucas started writing 1999's *Star Wars: Episode I—The Phantom Menace.* The first episode of the so-called Prequel Trilogy, it predates the story of *Star Wars,* which Lucas redubbed *Star Wars: Episode IV—A New Hope.* Despite his aversion to directing, Lucas once again took the helm. "As much as I wanted to hand over the last two films to other directors, I ended up being there all the time and I had to work as hard as if I were directing anyway," he said. "The other reason I wanted to direct *Episode I* was that we were going to be attempting new things; and, in truth, I didn't quite know how we were going to do them—nobody did."

Though *The Phantom Menace* was predictably a massive commercial success, it was widely considered an artistic disappointment—except when it came to its technical marvels. "The actors are wallpaper," *Rolling Stone* wrote, "the jokes are juvenile, there's no romance, and the dialogue lands with the thud of a computer-instruction manual." The character of Jar Jar Binks was particularly reviled by fans. "I'm sorry if they don't like it," Lucas said. "They should go back and see *The Matrix* or something."

In making *The Phantom Menace* and the two films that followed (2002's *Episode II—Attack of the Clones* and 2005's *Episode III—Revenge of the Sith*), Lucas introduced midi-chlorians, microscopic life-forms in the blood associated with the Force—an idea many fans found ludicrous. To make matters worse, the director had gotten sidetracked by technology. Sure, the visuals were breathtaking, but the heart was gone—along with the naivete that had given *Star Wars* its ineffable appeal. The man who'd claimed that engaging an audience was simple—all you had to do was

NATALIE PORTMAN AS PADMÉ Amidala, Queen of Naboo, in 1999's *The Phantom Menace* (above). Opposite: Lucas with R2-D2 and Jake Lloyd as Anakin Skywalker on the set of the same film. The first prequel was widely criticized, with the character of Jar Jar Binks proving particularly controversial, though Lucas maintains that Jar Jar is his favorite Star Wars character.

wring a kitten's neck—had gotten lost in machines.

It was one thing to produce a disappointing new product and another to mess with its beloved beginnings. Using the technology his company had developed, Lucas released a revamped "special edition" of *Star Wars* in 1997, adding digital effects—including Jabba the Hutt—and cleaning up some irritating glitches, such as the persistent shimmer beneath Luke's landspeeder. "It was basically a way to take this thorn out of my side and have the thing finished the way I originally wanted it to be finished," Lucas said.

The changes remain a sore spot with many viewers, however—especially since the original film is no longer available on DVD. "George," one Amazon customer recently wrote, "you caught lightning in a bottle not once, not twice, but THRICE. You should've left these alone, man!"

In 2012, Lucas sold the Star Wars franchise and Lucasfilm to Disney for $2.2 billion in cash and $1.855 billion in stock. The first Star Wars film made without Lucas's direct involvement, *The Force Awakens* was released in 2015. Though Lucas had hoped to continue the story of the midi-chlorians, taking the films into what he

YODA FIGHTS COUNT DOOKU in 2002's *Attack of the Clones* (above) and Hayden Christensen succumbs to the dark side in 2005's *Revenge of the Sith*. The Sith had been featured in Lucas's early drafts of 1977's *Star Wars*, in which Darth Vader was not a fallen Jedi but one of the Knights of the Sith.

"WHAT I ATTEMPTED WAS SCIENCE FICTION WITHOUT THE SCIENCE."

—GEORGE LUCAS

called "a microbiotic world," Disney ignored his story treatments in favor of the work of J.J. Abrams, who co-wrote and directed the film. Naturally, this didn't sit well with Lucas. Though he admitted that "a lot of fans would have hated" his approach, he disparaged *The Force Awakens* as "retro," claiming that dealing with Disney was like selling his children "to the white slavers."

Later, Lucas apologized. "George knew we weren't contractually bound to anything, but he thought that our buying the story treatments was a tacit promise that we'd follow them, and he was disappointed that his story was being discarded," Disney chairman and CEO Robert Iger wrote in his 2019 autobiography, *The Ride of a Lifetime: Lessons Learned from 15 Years as CEO of the Walt Disney Company.* "George felt betrayed, and while this whole process would never have been easy for him, we'd gotten off to an unnecessarily rocky start."

Though it's unclear if Lucas was involved in 2017's *The Last Jedi,* he was nominally consulted on the making of *The Rise of Skywalker,* the final installment of the Star Wars Skywalker Saga. "This movie had a very, very specific challenge, which was to take eight films and give an ending to three trilogies, and so we had to look at, what is the bigger story?" said Abrams, who once again co-wrote and directed. "We had conversations amongst ourselves, we met with George Lucas before we started writing the script."

NO MATTER WHAT LUCAS THINKS of the recent Star Wars installments, his legacy clearly extends far beyond the films. The Star Wars Universe has become a cultural touch point, with its lingo ("droids," "the dark side") entering the language. In the 1980s, President Ronald Reagan called his Strategic Defense Initiative "Star Wars" and referred to the Soviet Union as "the Evil Empire" (Lucasfilm sued for trademark infringement and lost). Not least, many have embraced the franchise's mystical concept of the Force as an actual belief system. In 2001, about 390,000 people in the United Kingdom called Jedi their religion—the fourth most popular in the survey.

Possibly Lucas's greatest influence lies in his pioneering approach to marketing. "In a way, this film was designed around toys," Lucas said before the first Star Wars film was released. "I actually make toys. I'm not making much for directing this movie. If I make money, it will be from the toys." A merchandising program that began with (among other things) R2-D2 cookie jars soon expanded to encompass trading cards, action figures, stormtrooper cuff links, and Darth Vader shower nozzles—just for starters. By 1981, *Star Wars* spin-offs had generated a reported $1 billion in sales.

But the heart of *Star Wars'* appeal

remains, well, its heart. "The humanity is what makes it," said Alan Ladd just after the film was released. "All I can say is that the man got a performance out of a robot." Make that *many* robots—not to mention a faceless villain in a black mask, a handful of cloaked dwarfs, and a Wookiee. "What I attempted was science fiction without the science," Lucas said. "I wanted an engaging Saturday matinee movie, but not camp or parody . . . There's a whole generation today with a great need for fantasy. The Lone Ranger and Long John Silver. *Star Wars* is hopefully a feeble attempt to make up for that lack, without goriness or violence."

The old-fashioned genre tropes are only part of *Star Wars'* pervasive nostalgia for a simpler—and seemingly better—time. Even the film's characters look longingly back on the good old days (Obi-Wan Kenobi calls the lightsaber "an elegant weapon for a more civilized age"). Four decades later, that nostalgia remains—for the film, if not its era. At a time when media is increasingly consumed alone and in private, anyone who first saw *Star Wars* in a dark theater—laughing, crying, and roaring with hundreds of strangers—will never forget the experience.

These days, the Star Wars Universe continues to attract new audiences, though not always through the films. There are Star Wars novels, comic books, websites, TV shows, video games—even an elaborate attraction called Galaxy's Edge, which opened at Disneyland this past May and at Walt Disney World in August. (Another attraction, the Rise of the Resistance, will open in December and January in Disney World and Disneyland, respectively.) What gives Star Wars its ongoing—and seemingly universal—appeal? In the 1970s, George Lucas saw a generation with "a great need for fantasy" and an even greater need for hope. In response, he created a modern myth in the form of a fairy tale. Then as now, we have a need for fantasy—and a need for hope. ●

LUCAS FRAMED A SCENE from *Revenge of the Sith* while Samuel L. Jackson looked on. The sixth episode in the Star Wars series, the film was generally well-received, though its dialogue was widely criticized. Lucas did not disagree with the assessment, calling himself "the king of wooden dialogue."

"THERE'S A WHOLE GENERATION TODAY WITH A GREAT NEED FOR FANTASY."

—GEORGE LUCAS

HARRISON FORD AND LUCAS signed autographs at the European premiere of *The Force Awakens* at London's Leicester Square in 2015. Increasingly, Lucas has found fame a burden. "You get harassed all the time," he said. "There are threats, letters from people whom you don't know, and you have to turn them over to the FBI."

PHOTO CREDITS

Front Cover: © Lucasfilm Ltd./20th Century Fox Film Corp., courtesy Photofest **Back Cover:** Sportsphoto/Alamy **Inside Cover and Page 1:** © Lucasfilm Ltd./ 20th Century Fox Film Corp., courtesy Photofest **Pages 2–3:** Lucasfilm/Fox/Kobal/Shutterstock

INTRODUCTION

Pages 4–5: Lucasfilm/AF Archive/Mary Evans

BEHIND THE SCENES

Pages 6–7: Lucasfilm/Fox/Kobal/Shutterstock **Pages 8–9:** Lucasfilm/AF Archive/Mary Evans **Pages 10–11:** United Archives GmbH/Alamy **Pages 12–13:** Lucasfilm Ltd./Paramount/ Kobal/Shutterstock **Pages 14–15:** "Lucasfilm Archives, Props and Set Pieces, Skywalker Ranch, Marin County, California." Taryn Simon, from *An American Index of the Hidden and Unfamiliar*, 2007. © Taryn Simon

A SHOOTING STAR

Pages 16–17: Modesto Bee/Zuma **Page 18:** Photo, McHenry Museum, Modesto, CA **Page 19:** Seth Poppel/Yearbook Library **Page 20:** Mary Evans **Page 21:** Seth Poppel/ Yearbook Library **Page 22:** Superstock/Everett **Page 23:** Courtesy Everett **Pages 24–25:** Dave Friedman (2) **Page 26:** Courtesy Everett **Page 27:** © 20th Century Fox Film Corp./ Courtesy Everett **Pages 28–29** (clockwise from left): Courtesy Everett (2); Toho/Kurosawa/ Kobal/Shutterstock **Pages 30–31:** Archive/ Moviepix/Getty **Page 31:** Silver Screen Collection/Moviepix/Getty **Pages 32–33:** © Warner Bros., courtesy Photofest **Page 34:** Warner Bros./Moviepix/Getty **Page 35:** Warner Bros./MPTVImages

AN *AMERICAN* AUTEUR

Pages 36–37: Universal Pictures/MPTVImages **Pages 38–39:** Dennis Stock/Magnum **Page 40:** Universal Pictures/MPTVImages **Pages 41–42:** Lucasfilm/Coppola Co./Universal/Kobal/ Shutterstock (2) **Page 43:** Universal Pictures/ MPTVImages **Pages 44–45:** Wayne Miller/ Magnum

***STAR WARS* IS BORN**

Pages 46–47: Bison Archives **Pages 48–49:** Steve Larson/The Denver Post/Getty **Pages 50–51:** © Lucasfilm Ltd./20th Century Fox Film Corp., courtesy Photofest **Page 52:** Terence Spencer/The LIFE Images Collection/ Getty **Pages 52–53:** Lucasfilm/Fox/Kobal/ Shutterstock **Page 54:** Colin Davey/Evening Standard/Hulton/Getty **Page 55:** Lucasfilm/AF Archive/Mary Evans **Page 56:** ITV/Shutterstock **Page 57:** Lucasfilm/AF Archive/Mary Evans **Page 58** (from top): © Paramount Pictures, courtesy Photofest; Courtesy Everett **Page 59:** Sunset Boulevard/Corbis/Getty **Pages 60–63:** Lucasfilm/Fox/Kobal/Shutterstock (4)

THE "IMPOSSIBLE" DREAM

Pages 64–65: © Lucasfilm Ltd./ 20th Century Fox Film Corp., courtesy Photofest **Pages 66–67:** AF Archive/Belstar Productions/Mary Evans **Page 68:** Lucasfilm/ AF Archive/Mary Evans **Pages 68–69:** Entertainment Pictures/Zuma **Pages 70–73:** Lucasfilm/Fox/Kobal/Shutterstock (2) **Pages 74–75:** Lucasfilm/AF Archive/Mary Evans **Pages 76–77:** © Lucasfilm Ltd./ 20th Century Fox Film Corp., courtesy Photofest **Page 78** (from top): Julian Wasser; Movie Poster Image Art/Moviepix/Getty **Pages 78–79:** Bison Archives **Pages 80–81:** Photofest

THE NEW HOLLYWOOD

Pages 82–83: Photo by Robert Sebree **Page 84:** Lucasfilm Ltd./Courtesy Everett **Page 85:** Terry Chostner/© Lucasfilm Ltd./20th Century Fox Film Corp., courtesy Photofest **Pages 86–87:** Lucasfilm/Fox/Kobal/Shutterstock **Page 88:** Keith Hamshere/Lucasfilm/Kobal/Shutterstock **Page 89:** Keith Hamshere/© Lucasfilm Ltd./20th Century Fox Film Corp., courtesy Photofest **Pages 90–91** (from top): 20th Century Fox Film Corp./Courtesy Everett; © Lucasfilm Ltd., courtesy Photofest **Pages 92–93:** Merrick Morton/© Lucasfilm Ltd., courtesy Photofest **Pages 94–95:** Dave J. Hogan/Getty **Page 96:** © 20th Century Fox Film Corp., courtesy Photofest

"MYTHS HELP YOU TO HAVE YOUR OWN HERO'S JOURNEY, FIND YOUR INDIVIDUALITY, FIND YOUR PLACE IN THE WORLD."

—GEORGE LUCAS

Made in United States
Orlando, FL
22 December 2021

12361434R10055